THE GOSPEL
OF JUDAS

Codex Tchacos in 2001

The Gospel of **Judas**

SECOND EDITION

EDITED BY **Rodolphe Kasser,**
Marvin Meyer, AND **Gregor Wurst**

IN COLLABORATION WITH **FRANÇOIS GAUDARD**

WITH ADDITIONAL COMMENTARY BY **BART D. EHRMAN,**
CRAIG A. EVANS, AND **GESINE SCHENKE ROBINSON**

NATIONAL GEOGRAPHIC
WASHINGTON, D.C.

Published by the National Geographic Society
1145 17th Street, N.W., Washington, D.C. 20036-4688

ISBN: 978-1-4262-0048-9

Library of Congress Cataloging-in-Publication Data available on request.

Defining Time Periods
Many scholars and editors working today in the multicultural discipline of
world history use terminology that does not impose the standards of one cul-
ture on others. As recommended by the scholars who have contributed to the
National Geographic Society's publication of the Gospel of Judas, this book
uses the terms BCE (before the Common Era) and CE (Common Era). BCE
refers to the same time period as B.C. (before Christ), and CE refers to the
same time period as A.D. (anno Domini, a Latin phrase meaning "in the year
of the Lord").

Founded in 1888, the National Geographic Society is one of the largest nonprofit
scientific and educational organizations in the world. It reaches more than 285 million
people worldwide each month through its official journal, NATIONAL GEOGRAPHIC,
and its four other magazines; the National Geographic Channel; television documentaries; radio programs; films; books; videos and DVDs; maps; and interactive media.
National Geographic has funded more than 8,000 scientific research projects and
supports an education program combating geographic illiteracy.

For more information, please call 1-800-NGS LINE (647-5463), write to the Society at
the above address, or visit us online at www.nationalgeographic.com.

Photographs by Kenneth Garrett

Interior design: Cameron Zotter
Design assistant: Al Morrow

Printed in the U.S.A.

CONTENTS

The concluding page of the Gospel of Judas

INTRODUCTION

OVER THE YEARS THE SANDS OF EGYPT HAVE SURRENDERED COUNTLESS treasures and archaeological wonders, and now they have yielded another spectacular find—the Gospel of Judas, recently discovered and published for the first time in 2006.

The very title of the text, the Gospel of Judas—Judas Iscariot—is shocking. In the New Testament gospels and most of the Christian tradition, Judas Iscariot is portrayed as the quintessential traitor, the betrayer of Jesus, who turns his master in to the Roman authorities. According to these accounts, there is little that is apparent in his character that could connect him with the gospel, or "good news," of Jesus. In the Gospel of Luke, it is said that Satan enters into Judas and drives him to his despicable deed, and in the Gospel of John, Jesus addresses the twelve disciples and says that one of them, Judas, is a devil. The end of Judas is as ignominious as his actions. He takes blood money from the authorities for his betrayal of Jesus, and either he hangs himself (as in Matthew) or he dies in a ghastly fashion (as in Acts), falling headlong and causing his belly to rip open.

Yet, even in the New Testament, there is something captivating about Judas Iscariot. The account of Judas betraying

Jesus remains a story of great power and poignancy: Jesus is handed over by one of his closest friends. Furthermore, in the New Testament gospels, there are hints of a more favorable figure of Judas Iscariot. Judas is part of the inner circle of disciples of Jesus, and according to the Gospel of John, Judas acts as the treasurer of the group and is entrusted with whatever funds Jesus and the disciples might have had. At the Last Supper, Jesus himself tells Judas to do what he has to do and to do it quickly. Judas kisses Jesus in the garden, with a form of greeting still used today between friends throughout the Middle East. Wasn't all this part of the divine plan, according to the New Testament—that Jesus should die for the sins of people and rise from the dead on the third day? Without Judas and his kiss, would the crucifixion and resurrection ever have taken place?

The enigma of Judas Iscariot has been explored by many who have wondered about Judas's character and motivation. Modern literature and academic scholarship are rich with discussions of Judas, including Jorge Luis Borges's *Three Versions of Judas*, Mikhail Bulgakov's *The Master and Margarita*, Hans-Josef Klauck's *Judas: Ein Jünger des Herrn*, William Klassen's *Judas: Betrayer or Friend of Jesus?*, Hyam Maccoby's *Judas Iscariot and the Myth of Jewish Evil*, and Marcel Pagnol's play, *Judas*. In the rock musical *Jesus Christ Superstar*, Judas Iscariot nearly steals the show, and his presence and music provide a more sympathetic view of the depth of his devotion to Jesus. In the song "With God on Our Side," Bob Dylan sings of Judas:

You'll have to decide
Whether Judas Iscariot
Had God on his side.

The Judas Iscariot of the Gospel of Judas is the one who betrays Jesus, but he is simultaneously the protagonist of the gospel. He says to Jesus, "I know who you are and where you have come from. You have come from the immortal aeon of Barbelo. And I am not worthy to utter the name of the one who has sent you." In the spiritual world of the Gospel of Judas, to confess that Jesus is from "the immortal aeon of Barbelo" is to confess that he is a divine being, and to declare the ineffability of the name of the one who sent Jesus is to profess that the true God is the infinite Spirit of the universe. Unlike the other disciples, who misunderstand Jesus and cannot bear to stand before his face, Judas understands who Jesus is, takes his place before him, and learns from him.

In the end, Judas hands Jesus over in the Gospel of Judas, but he does so knowingly, after being fully informed by Jesus. Jesus says to Judas, with reference to the other disciples, "You will exceed all of them. For you will sacrifice the man who bears me." According to the Gospel of Judas, Jesus is a savior not because of the mortal flesh that he wears but because he can reveal the soul or spiritual person who is within, and the true home of Jesus is not this imperfect world below but the divine world of light and life. For Jesus in the Gospel of Judas, death is no tragedy, nor is it an evil necessary to bring about the forgiveness of sins. As a result, the act of Judas handing Jesus over to be crucified in the Gospel of Judas loses a great deal of the negative meaning and significance ordinarily associated with it.

Unlike the New Testament gospels, the Jesus of the Gospel of Judas laughs a great deal, and part of that laughter is directed toward the foibles of the disciples and the absurdities in human life. Death, as the exit from the absurdity of physical existence, is not to be feared or dreaded. Far from being an occasion of sadness, death is the means by which Jesus is liberated from the flesh in order that he might return to his heavenly home. Jesus will be handed over by Judas, but this will provide the occasion for Jesus to discard his body and free his inner self, the divine self. No wonder Jesus laughs.

This perspective of the Gospel of Judas is different in a number of respects from that of the New Testament gospels. During the formative period of the Christian church, numerous gospels were composed in addition to the canonical gospels of Matthew, Mark, Luke, and John. Among the other gospels that have survived, whole or in part, are the Gospel of Truth and the Gospels of Thomas, Peter, Philip, Mary, the Ebionites, the Nazoreans, the Hebrews, and the Egyptians, to name a few, and these gospels demonstrate the rich diversity of perspectives within early Christianity. The Gospel of Judas is yet another of the gospels written by early Christians as they attempted to articulate, in one way or another, who Jesus is and how one should follow him.

THE DISCOVERY

The Gospel of Judas was discovered in the 1970s in Middle Egypt in a papyrus codex (or book), later designated Codex Tchacos. According to reports, the codex was found, with other manuscripts, in a cave that had been used for a burial. It was apparently displayed, stolen, and later recovered, and the collection of manuscripts was taken to Europe and presented to scholars with a view to a sale, though the suggested purchase price proved prohibitively high. Eventually the Gospel of Judas made its way to the United States, where it was hidden away in a safe-deposit box on Long Island for sixteen years and then was placed in a freezer by a potential buyer. By the time the codex was acquired by the Maecenas Foundation for Ancient Art and the National Geographic Society, for conservation and publication, this much-abused book consisted of a mass of fragments in a box. Beginning in 2001, Rodolphe Kasser undertook—with conservator Florence Darbre and, since 2004, Gregor Wurst—the Herculean task of assembling and arranging the papyrus fragments, large and small. In time, mirabile dictu, the box of fragments became an ancient collection of books once again.

As preserved, Codex Tchacos is at least sixty-six pages long and contains at least four tractates:

- a version of the Letter of Peter to Philip (pages 1-9), also known from Nag Hammadi Codex VIII
- a text entitled James (pages 10-30), which is a version of the First Revelation of James from Nag Hammadi Codex V
- the Gospel of Judas (pages 33-58)
- a text provisionally entitled the Book of Allogenes (or, the Stranger, an epithet of Seth, son of Adam and Eve, in gnostic texts), previously unknown (pages 59-66).

A papyrus fragment of Codex Tchacos has also been discovered that seems to contain the page number 108, and Jean-Pierre Mahé has identified among the remaining papyrus fragments what he believes are words and phrases that come from a Coptic translation of a famous Hermetic text, Corpus Hermeticum XIII. Thus, Codex Tchacos may once have been a larger book than we might have imagined, and unless any remaining papyrus fragments have turned to dust, it is conceivable that there may be more fragments, and even more pages, of the ancient collection still to be discovered.

Although the Gospel of Judas and the other texts in the codex are written in Coptic, a late form of the ancient Egyptian language, the Gospel of Judas was, without a doubt, originally composed in Greek, probably around the middle of the second century. This date becomes more secure on the basis of a statement of Irenaeus of Lyon, who refers to a Gospel of Judas in his work *Against Heresies,* written around 180. As Gregor Wurst demonstrates in his essay, the Gospel of Judas in the Codex Tchacos may now be identified as a version of the Gospel of Judas mentioned by Irenaeus and others after him. The Coptic translation of the Gospel of Judas is most likely somewhat older than the copy we find in Codex Tchacos, which probably dates to the early part of the fourth century, though the carbon-14 dating would also allow for a slightly earlier date for the codex.

THE GNOSTIC CONTEXT

The Gospel of Judas may be classified as what is often called a gnostic gospel. Probably composed around the mid-second century, as noted, most likely on the basis of earlier ideas and sources, the Gospel of Judas represents an early form of spirituality that emphasizes *gnōsis,* or "knowledge"—mystical knowledge, knowledge of God, and the essential oneness of the self with God. This spirituality is commonly described as "gnostic," but there was a debate in the ancient world over the use of the term, and that debate goes on to the present day among scholars. Such a direct approach to God as is to be found in gnostic spirituality requires no intermediary—after all, God is the spirit and light within.

Evidence from the early church and the heresiologists (heresy hunters) within the church indicates that the priests and bishops were not pleased with these freethinking gnostics. The writings of the heresiologists are filled with accusations that gnostics entertained evil thoughts and engaged in illicit activities. Polemics is not a pretty business, and documents with polemical intentions, such as those of the heresiologists, frequently try to discredit their opponents by raising suspicions about their thought and life. The gnostic Gospel of Judas returns the favor by accusing the leaders and members of the emerging orthodox church of all sorts of unsavory behavior. According to the Gospel of Judas, these rival Christians are simply lackeys of the God who rules this world below, and their lives reflect his disgusting ways.

The Gospel of Judas makes mention of Seth, well-known from the biblical book of Genesis, and concludes that human beings with the knowledge of God belong to the generation of Seth. This particular form of gnostic thought is often described by scholars as Sethian. In the story told in the book of Genesis, Seth, third son of Adam and Eve, was born after the tragic violence in the dysfunctional first family, which left Abel dead and Cain banished. Seth, it is suggested, represents a new beginning for humanity. To belong to the generation of Seth, then, according to the Gospel of Judas and similar Sethian books, is to be part of enlightened humanity. That is the good news of salvation in Sethian texts like the Gospel of Judas.

In the central part of this gospel, Jesus teaches Judas the mysteries of the universe. In the Gospel of Judas, as in other gnostic gospels, Jesus is primarily a teacher and revealer of wisdom and knowledge, not a savior who dies for the sins of the world. For gnostics, the fundamental problem in human life is not sin but ignorance, and the best way to address this problem is not through faith but through knowledge. In the Gospel of Judas, Jesus imparts to Judas—and to the readers of the gospel—the knowledge that can eradicate ignorance and lead to an awareness of oneself and God.

This revelatory section of the Gospel of Judas, however, may present challenges to modern readers. The challenges arise chiefly because the point of view of the Sethian gnostic revelation differs substantially from the philosophy, theology, and cosmology that we have inherited within the Euro-American tradition. Rome and orthodox Christianity eventually won the day, and as Borges once noted concerning the gnostic accounts he was discussing, "Had Alexandria triumphed and not Rome, the extravagant and muddled stories that I have summarized here would be coherent, majestic, and perfectly ordinary." The gnostics of Alexandria and Egypt did not triumph, nor did the Gospel of Judas, in the theological wars that raged during the second, third, and fourth centuries, and consequently texts like the Gospel of Judas, with their different perspectives, contain ideas that sound unusual today.

Nonetheless, the revelation that Jesus imparts to Judas in the Gospel of Judas illustrates a theology and cosmology that are still quite sophisticated. The revelation itself contains few Christian elements, and, if scholars are correct in their understanding of the development of gnostic traditions, the roots of these ideas may go back to the first century or even before, within Jewish philosophical and gnostic circles that were open to Greco-Roman ideas. Jesus tells Judas that in the beginning there was an infinite, utterly transcendent deity, and through a complex series of emanations and creations, the heavens became filled with divine light and glory. This infinite deity is so exalted that no finite term can adequately describe the deity; even the word *God,* it is intimated, is insufficient and inappropriate for the deity. The world below, however, is the domain of a lower ruler, a creator God named Nebro ("Rebel") or Yaldabaoth, who is malevolent and mean-spirited—hence the problems in our world and hence the need to listen to words of wisdom and become aware of the divine light within.

For these believers, the most profound mystery of the universe is that within some human beings is the spirit of the divine. Although we live in a flawed world that too often is the domain of darkness and death, we can transcend darkness and embrace life. We are better than this world, Jesus explains to Judas, for we belong to the world of the divine. If Jesus is the son of the divine, so also are all of us children of the divine. All we need to do is live out of that knowledge of the divine, and we shall be enlightened.

In contrast to the New Testament gospels, Judas Iscariot is presented in an unfamiliar and rather unorthodox way in the Gospel of Judas, a way that shows what it means in this world for the wisdom and knowledge of God to be present and for a person of knowledge to be a disciple of Jesus. The Gospel of Judas describes the vicissitudes of Judas, who is opposed and persecuted but nonetheless is informed of everything by Jesus. The story of the Gospel of Judas ends as Judas does exactly what Jesus says he will do, with the handing over of Jesus and not the crucifixion. The point of the gospel is that Jesus is a savior not because of a sacrificial death that he experiences but rather because of the wisdom and knowledge that he reveals—the very knowledge that he reveals to Judas in the Gospel of Judas.

In the biblical tradition, however, Judas—whose name has been linked to "Jew" and "Judaism"—was often portrayed chiefly as the evil Jew who turned Jesus in to be arrested and killed, and thereby the biblical figure of Judas the betrayer has fed the flames of anti-Semitism. The role of Judas in the present gospel, along with the more positive hints about the character of Judas in the New Testament gospels, may help to counteract this anti-Semitic tendency. In the Gospel of Judas, Judas Iscariot turns out to be the one disciple of Jesus who truly understands who he is, and Jesus singles him out for further discussion of the true nature of the divine, the cosmos, and salvation. Additionally, the mysteries Judas learns from Jesus are steeped in Jewish mystical lore, and the teacher of these mysteries, Jesus, is the master. The Christian Gospel of Judas is at peace with a Jewish view—an alternative Jewish view, to be sure—of gnostic thought, and Jewish gnostic thought has been baptized as Christian gnostic thought.

In this book, Jesus echoes the Platonic conviction that every person has his or her own star and that the fate of people is connected to their stars. Judas, Jesus says, also has his star. Near the conclusion of the text, just before an account of transfiguration in a luminous cloud, Jesus asks Judas to look up at the heavens and see the stars and the display of light. There are many stars in the sky, but the star of Judas is said to be special. Jesus tells Judas, "The star that leads the way is your star."

THE RECEPTION OF THE GOSPEL OF JUDAS

Since the initial publication of the Gospel of Judas, there has been an extraordinary outpouring of interest in the text on the part of the general public as well as scholars of early Christianity and gnostic spirituality. In April 2006, the National Geographic Society published the first edition of *The Gospel of Judas*—edited by Rodolphe Kasser, Marvin Meyer, Gregor Wurst, and François Gaudard—and simultaneously provided a provisional transcription of the Coptic manuscript on its Web site in an effort to make a text and translation—if a provisional text and translation—available to the public and to scholars in as timely a manner as possible. At the same time, the story of the discovery of the Gospel of Judas and Codex Tchacos was published in *The Lost Gospel: The Quest for the Gospel of Judas Iscariot,* by Herbert Krosney, and in a popular article, with photographs, in NATIONAL GEOGRAPHIC magazine. A television documentary about the discovery, restoration, and significance of the Gospel of Judas also aired on the National Geographic Channel.

The Society followed up these initial publications in June 2007 with a scholarly critical edition of the Gospel of Judas and the three other extant texts that make up Codex Tchacos. This new edition was edited by Rodolphe Kasser, Marvin Meyer, Gregor Wurst, and François Gaudard and included color photographs of the papyrus pages of Codex Tchacos, a revised transcription of the Coptic text, translations in English and French, textual notes, introductions to each of the texts, and an essay on features of the Coptic dialect of the codex. High-resolution photographs of Codex Tchacos have since been made available on the National Geographic's Web site (*ftp://ftp10.nationalgeographic.com*), for the use of Coptic scholars around the world in the ongoing research on this remarkable text and codex.

The formal announcement of the appearance of the Gospel of Judas, made by the National Geographic Society and the Maecenas Foundation, prompted an immediate response on the part of the media around the world, and most of the major newspapers worldwide carried significant and often front-page stories about the Gospel of Judas in the days following the announcement. Prominent journalists, some of whom are better known for their secular interests than their religious interests, were moved to comment on the text in leading periodicals, and letters, telephone calls, and e-mail messages began to pour in from people who wished to find out more about the Gospel of Judas. A number of church leaders responded to the publication of the text, often with enthusiasm about the historical importance of the text, sometimes with statements highlighting the heretical nature of the text, in keeping with the views of writers in the early church, such as Irenaeus of Lyon. Scholars were contacted for interviews, and many gave lectures on the Gospel of Judas throughout the world, often to large and engaged audiences. Some scholars, however, were critical of the National Geographic Society and the Maecenas Foundation because of the limited access to the manuscript during the conservation, editing, and translation process.

The first edition of the Gospel of Judas was translated into many languages, and other translations and studies of the gospel quickly appeared. The editorial team preparing the critical edition presented its work at scholarly conferences at the Sorbonne in Paris and at the annual meeting of the American Academy of Religion and the Society of Biblical Literature in Washington, D.C., both in the fall of 2006. At these conferences, up-to-date versions of the Coptic transcription of the Gospel of Judas were distributed to all who wished to receive them. The National Geographic team continued to solicit the input of colleagues on the Coptic text, and the discussion about it has not diminished.

Now that the critical edition has been published (updating the earlier transcription available online) and photographs of the manuscript pages have been made available, scholars are weighing in with various interpretations of the text and providing their own translations. The early books on the Gospel of Judas—including the National Geographic first edition of *The Gospel of Judas,* Bart Ehrman's *Lost Gospel of Judas Iscariot:*

A New Look at Betrayer and Betrayed, and Elaine Pagels and
Karen L. King's *Reading Judas: The Gospel of Judas and the
Shaping of Christianity,* among others—have recognized the
surprisingly favorable portrayal of Judas Iscariot in the text,
which is, after all, entitled the Gospel, or "good news," of
Judas. It is Judas who, from a Sethian gnostic perspective,
has the correct confession of who Jesus is and who receives
the central cosmological teaching from Jesus. Indeed, Judas is
the one who is said to have heard the mysteries of the kingdom from Jesus. At the end of the gospel Judas hands over
the man who bears Jesus to the authorities, but that figure is
the mortal body of Jesus, not the true, inner person of Jesus.
Furthermore, it has been pointed out that Irenaeus of Lyon,
who knew of the Gospel of Judas, was outraged by the text.
Irenaeus charges that Judas is favored in this gospel as the one
who knows the truth, beyond the others, and he understands
that the Gospel of Judas proclaims a different sort of betrayal
of Jesus by Judas, an act he calls the mystery of the betrayal.

In subsequent studies of the Gospel of Judas, however,
some scholars have emphasized other passages in the text that
are more ambivalent about the person of Judas Iscariot, and
they have opposed any consideration of a rehabilitated and
redeemed figure of Judas in the Gospel of Judas. As a more
definitive Coptic text emerged after the preliminary transcription, a few new readings of passages were accepted and presented in the critical edition. For example, on the bottom of
manuscript page 35 of the Gospel of Judas, the preliminary
Coptic transcription yielded this translation in 2006: "It is
possible for you to reach it (i.e., the kingdom), but you will
grieve a great deal." Now, after careful examination of the ink
traces in this passage, the National Geographic team has suggested a new Coptic transcription in the critical edition, with

this translation: ". . . not so that you will go there (i.e., to the kingdom), but you will grieve a great deal." Also, on the bottom of manuscript page 46 and the top of page 47, the preliminary Coptic transcription produced this translation in 2006: "In the last days they will curse your ascent to the holy [generation]," with the accompanying note that the translation is tentative. The new transcription in the critical edition provides the basis for this translation: "In the last days they <will . . . > to you, and you will not ascend on high to the holy [generation]." Even with this translation, however, a textual error has been assumed to have taken place, with words having been inadvertently left out, so that the passage remains very problematic. Still, both of these new readings may be taken to intimate that Judas is not able to ascend on high but is destined to be detained in this mortal realm.

Other scholars go further in identifying what they judge to be other passages in the Gospel of Judas that portray Judas in an unfavorable light. They see the stars, for instance, as being entirely hostile in the text, so that when Jesus says to Judas, "The star that leads the way is your star," that is hardly a good thing. Moreover, if Judas is to attain the thirteenth realm, or aeon, some scholars assume that statement to be an admission that Judas is in league with the demiurge, the grim creator of this world—Nebro or Yaldabaoth—who sometimes is thought to reside in the thirteenth aeon and rule from there over the twelve cosmic realms below him. For that reason, some have concluded, when Judas is called the "thirteenth daimon" in the Gospel of Judas, he is not the thirteenth "spirit," with a Greco-Roman understanding of the word of Greek derivation, but an actual "demon," or evil spirit.

Along these lines, a number of scholars have produced revisionist interpretations of the text, according to which they highlight what they presume to be a tragic element in the gospel. Maybe Judas does not attain bliss after all in the Gospel of Judas. Perhaps he is presented as a wicked demon. And when Jesus says to Judas, in a passage marked by lacunae, or gaps in the text, "You will exceed all of them," he may mean that Judas will surpass all the other disciples in evil. Birger Pearson has written, "If Judas Iscariot can be called the 'hero' of the Gospel of Judas, I would suggest that he is a tragic hero." Other scholars—Louis Painchaud, Gesine Schenke Robinson, and John D. Turner, among others—have voiced similar sentiments; Painchaud suggests that the text uses the betrayer Judas to warn gnostics against apostasy, that is, defecting to the apostolic church and its sacrificial rituals.

April DeConick, in her book *The Thirteenth Apostle: What the Gospel of Judas Really Says*, not only considers Judas to be a tragic figure; she considers the Gospel of Judas to be a gospel parody. DeConick is convinced that Judas is the thirteenth demon, "the wickedest of all men" in the Gospel of Judas, and if he knows who Jesus is, it is simply because demons are able to recognize Jesus. If he is instructed by Jesus, it is part of a mischievous ploy on the part of Jesus, and thereby Jesus shows Judas how awful his alliance is with the demiurge and how horrific his fate. If he sacrifices the man who bears Jesus, he is responsible, ignorantly, for the perpetuation of the violent cult of sacrificial atonement. Judas is Yaldabaoth's boy, a stooge of the archons or rulers of this world, and no role model for gnostics. DeConick concludes:

> What does the Gospel of Judas really say? If we follow the story-line from beginning to end, what it means is different depending on your perspective. If you are Judas, it is a story of tragedy, of a human being who became entangled in the snares of the archons

who rule this world. If you are an apostolic Christian, it is a story of ridicule, a representation of your faith as based on faithless apostles and a demon-sponsored atonement. If you are a Sethian Christian, it is a story of humor, of laughter at the ignorance of Christians not in the know.

Since the appearance of DeConick's book, I have explored the use of the terms "thirteenth aeon" and "daimon" in the world of gnostic literature, and I have turned up new data and a new approach to the evaluation of these themes in the Gospel of Judas, which raise questions about this view. Evidence in Irenaeus of Lyon and a gnostic text entitled Pistis Sophia suggests a possible connection between Judas and the figure of Sophia, or divine Wisdom, reflected in the Gospel of Judas (see my essay below, pages 125-154). In the end, I suspect that in the future the figure of Judas Iscariot in the Gospel of Judas may be interpreted, in good Hegelian fashion—and in the light of such parallel texts—as neither a completely positive character nor a totally demonic being, but rather a figure, like Sophia, and like any gnostic, who is embroiled in this world of mortality yet is striving for gnosis and enlightenment.

That the study of the Gospel of Judas has produced such different interpretations may initially come as a surprise, until several features of the text and scholarly work on the text are recalled. The manuscript of Codex Tchacos, though largely reconstructed, remains difficult to understand, and as the fates—or archons—would have it, Coptic text is missing at key places in the manuscript, particularly near the conclusion of the Gospel of Judas. Unless more text is recovered and papyrus fragments are found and placed, it may prove difficult to resolve, once and for all, questions about Judas and the overall message of the text. The Coptic text that is legible is frequently challenging to translate and interpret, and ambiguous passages abound.

Part of the reason for the interpretive divide among scholars studying the Gospel of Judas can also be traced back to different strategies for understanding the text. Some scholars perceive the text as an early gospel that shows a Christian Sethian perspective in a developmental stage, and so the Greco-Roman and Jewish elements observed in the text may take on an early form. Others interpret the text as a gospel with Sethian characteristics that can best be explained from other Sethian texts found in the Nag Hammadi library and elsewhere. Further, there simply seem to be, at face value, different statements about Judas and evaluations of Judas in the text, and some scholars gravitate to one set of statements, other scholars to another set. At stake in the divergent interpretations of the Gospel of Judas is the very nature of the text. Who is Jesus in the text and who is Judas? What is the purpose of the text? Is the gospel fundamentally *evangelium* or *dysangelium,* good news or bad news? What does the Gospel of Judas really mean?

The discussion of the meaning of the Gospel of Judas is exciting and dynamic, and it is certain to continue into the future. Scholars will continue to scrutinize the reconstruction of the codex and the placement of fragments, and they will propose new textual restorations and new readings. Unplaced fragments may be placed; missing papyrus may be found. New suggestions for translation and interpretation will be presented and debated, and new theories will be advanced. In a way, the work on the Gospel of Judas has only begun. In the months and years ahead, more light will undoubtedly be shed on this fascinating gospel of light.

ABOUT THIS EDITION

The English translation of the Gospel of Judas published here is based on the collaborative work of Rodolphe Kasser, myself, Gregor Wurst, and François Gaudard, as well as the input from other scholars who have offered additional suggestions for translation and interpretation. A consensus English translation of the recovered text of the Gospel of Judas, with which all the translators were in essential agreement, was published as the first edition of this book in 2006 and was later revised and updated in 2007 for the critical edition.

The English translation of this second, expanded edition reproduces—with a few new readings, improvements in style, and modifications in translation—the English translation incorporated into the critical edition. A small number of fragments have been placed since the publication of the critical edition in 2007, and most often they affect only the use of square brackets (that is, the degree of a restoration) in the translation. In a few instances, additional words have been restored and incorporated into the translation.

The current translation is intended to be, as much as is possible, a neutral one, not presupposing any particular interpretation but leaving room for a diversity of interpretations. Some of the most significant alternative translations are included in the footnotes, as are different interpretive points. We anticipate that the present translation retains, as is the case with any translation, a provisional character, and we look forward to more suggestions for translation and interpretation as the scholarly work on the Gospel of Judas continues.

The translation of the Gospel of Judas is presented here in such a way as to enhance the understanding of the text. Subtitles within the translation, not found in the text itself, are provided by the translators in order to clarify the translation, structure, and flow of the text. The numbers of the manuscript pages are given in square brackets, [ ], and in the accompanying discussions, sections of the text are referred to by these page numbers. Square brackets are also used to indicate lacunae (gaps in the text owing to the loss of ink or loss of papyrus), with restorations of lacunae placed within the brackets. Some names or words that are partially restored are placed partly inside and partly outside square brackets in order to indicate the portion of the name or word that survives in the manuscript.

When a short lacuna of less than a manuscript line cannot be restored with confidence, three ellipsis dots are placed within the brackets, [. . .]. For unrestored lacunae longer than a fraction of a manuscript line, the approximate number of missing lines is indicated within the square brackets. Because of the fragmentary nature of the manuscript and portions of the text that remain unaccounted for, there are several rather long lacunae, with a substantial number of lines missing. Once in a while, angle brackets, < >, are used for an emendation of an apparent error in the text. Alternative translations and particular issues of translation are indicated in the footnotes.

Following the translation are essays by Rodolphe Kasser, Bart D. Ehrman, Craig A. Evans, myself, Gesine Schenke Robinson, and Gregor Wurst, each offering commentary from one point of view or another on the meaning and significance of the text. These essays expand upon the concerns that arise in the Gospel of Judas and help to clarify various points of interpretation. Some of the essays include notes, published at the end of this volume, with suggestions for further inquiry and reading.

After being lost for 1,600 years or more, the Gospel of Judas has at last been found. The authors of this volume hope that the Gospel of Judas may contribute to our knowledge and appreciation of the history, development, and diversity of the early Christian church and shed light on the enduring issues it faced during that formative period.

—MARVIN MEYER
January 2008

THE GOSPEL OF JUDAS

The opening page of the Gospel of Judas

THE GOSPEL OF JUDAS

Translated by Rodolphe Kasser, Marvin Meyer,
Gregor Wurst, and François Gaudard

INTRODUCTION: INCIPIT

The secret word[1] of declaration[2] by which Jesus spoke in con-versation with Judas Iscariot, during eight days,[3] three days before he celebrated Passover.[4]

THE EARTHLY MINISTRY OF JESUS

When he appeared on earth, he performed miracles and great wonders for the salvation of humanity. And since some

---

1. Or, "account," "treatise" (Coptic, from Greek, *logos*). A substantial number of words of Greek derivation are included in the Coptic text of the Gospel of Judas as loanwords.
2. Or, "exposition," "revelation" (Coptic, from Greek, *apophasis*). In his *Refutation of All Heresies* 6.9.4–18.7, Hippolytus of Rome cites another work, attributed to Simon Magus, that employs the same Greek term in its title: *Apophasis megalē*, "Great Revelation" (or "Declaration, Exposition"). Here Jacques van der Vliet and Gesine Schenke Robinson prefer to translate the opening phrase "The secret declaration of judgment," "The secret doctrine of the verdict," or the like, with reference to the final eschatological judgment against the emerging orthodox church. André Gagné suggests "The secret word of the denial," with reference to the denial of true salvation for Judas. The titular subscript, "The Gospel of Judas," is found at the end of the text.
3. The phrase "during eight days" may be intended to indicate a week.
4. Or, "three days before his passion." The Gospel of Judas chronicles events described as taking place over a short period of time leading up to the betrayal of Jesus by Judas. In the New Testament see Matthew 21:1–26:56; Mark 11:1–14:52; Luke 19:28–22:53; John 12:12–18:11.

[walked] in the way of righteousness while others walked in their transgression, the twelve disciples were called.[5]

He began to speak with them about the mysteries[6] beyond the world and what would take place at the end. But often he does not appear to his disciples (as himself), but you find[7] him among them . . .[8]

JESUS CONVERSES WITH HIS DISCIPLES

One day he was with his disciples in Judea, and he found them seated and gathered together practicing their piety.[9] When he [approached] his disciples, [34] gathered together and seated and offering a prayer of thanksgiving[10] over the bread, [he] laughed.[11]

---

5. On the calling of the twelve disciples, see Matthew 10:1-4; Mark 3:13-19; Luke 6:12-16. Here Peter Nagel and Gesine Schenke Robinson suggest that the verb may be emended to read "<he> called the twelve disciples."

6. Coptic, from Greek, *mmustērion*, here and below.

7. Peter Nagel and Gesine Schenke Robinson propose that this be emended to read "<they> find"; Hans-Gebhard Bethge and Uwe-Karsten Plisch consider this entire sentence to be a secondary gloss.

8. Perhaps read "as a child" or "an apparition" or even "a veil." The meaning of *ʿnhrot* is unclear. The Coptic word *hrot* may be taken as a form of the Bohairic Coptic word *hrot*, "child," or a form of the Bohairic Coptic word *hortf*, "apparition," or even a form of the Sahidic Coptic word *šort*, "veil." On Jesus appearing as a child, see the Secret Book of John (Nag Hammadi Codex II), 2; Revelation of Paul 18; Acts of John 88; Hippolytus of Rome, *Refutation of All Heresies* 6.42.2, where Hippolytus reports a story that the Word (Logos) appeared to Valentinus as a child; Gospel of Thomas 4; etc. On Jesus appearing as an apparition, see the Acts of John; the Second Discourse of Great Seth; the Nag Hammadi Revelation of Peter; etc. John D. Turner and April DeConick translate this phrase "when necessary" (emending the text to read *ʿnhtor*).

9. Literally, "training their piety" (Coptic, partly from Greek, *euʿrgumnaze etmntnoute*; see 1 Timothy 4:7).

10. Coptic, from Greek, *euʿreukharisti*.

11. The scene recalls, in part, accounts of the last supper, particularly the blessing over the bread, or descriptions of some other holy meal within Judaism and Christianity. The specific language used here also calls to mind the celebration of the Eucharist within Christianity. Note here the additional criticisms within the Gospel of Judas of sacrifice and forms of worship within the emerging orthodox church. On Jesus laughing, see the Secret Book of John; Wisdom of Jesus Christ III:91-92;

[And] the disciples said to him, "Master, why are you laughing at [our] prayer of thanksgiving?[12] Or what did we do? [This] is what is right."

He answered and said to them, "I am not laughing at you. You are not doing this because of your own will but because it is through this that your God [will receive] thanksgiving."[13]

They said, "Master, you [. . .] are the son of our God."[14]

Jesus said to them, "In what way do [you] know me? Truly [I] say to you,[15] no generation of the people that are among you will know me."[16]

THE DISCIPLES BECOME ANGRY

When his disciples heard this, [they] started getting angry and infuriated, and began blaspheming against him in their hearts.

And when Jesus observed their lack of understanding, [he said] to them, "Why has this agitation led (you) to anger? Your God who is within you and [his . . .][17] [35] have become angry together with your souls. [Let] any one of you who is

---

Second Discourse of Great Seth 56; Revelation of Peter 81; Basilides, in Irenaeus of Lyon, *Against Heresies* 1.24.4; and several other passages in the Gospel of Judas.

12. Or, "eucharist" (Coptic, from Greek, *eukharistia*).

13. Or, "[will be] praised." The God described as the God of the disciples is not the exalted deity above but rather the ruler of this world.

14. See the confession of Peter in Matthew 16:13-20, Mark 8:27-30, and Luke 9:18-21. Here, however, the disciples mistakenly confess that Jesus is the son of their own God. Hans-Gebhard Bethge and Peter Nagel suggest restoring the lacuna to read [*pjois*], to be translated "You, [O Lord], are the son of our God," or "You are [the Lord], the son of our God."

15. Or, "Amen [I] say to you." This is the standard introductory statement of authority in sayings of Jesus in early Christian literature. Here and elsewhere in the Gospel of Judas, the statement is given with the Coptic *hamēn* (from the Hebrew *amen*).

16. In the Gospel of Judas and other Sethian texts, the human generations are distinguished from "that generation" (Coptic *tgenea etʻmmau*), the great generation of Seth—that is, the gnostics. Elsewhere in Sethian literature—for example, in the Revelation of Adam—the people of Seth can similarly be described as "those people" (Coptic *nirōme etʻmmau*).

17. Perhaps restore to read "[his powers]," "[his lackeys]," or the like.

[strong enough] among human beings bring out the perfect human and stand before my face."[18]

And they all said, "We have the strength."

But their spirits[19] could not find the courage to stand before [him], except for Judas Iscariot. He was able to stand before him, but he could not look him in the eyes, and he turned his face away.[20]

Judas said to him, "I know who you are and where you have come from. You have come from the immortal aeon[21] of Barbelo.[22] And I am not worthy to utter the name of the one who has sent you."[23]

JESUS SPEAKS TO JUDAS PRIVATELY

Knowing that he (Judas) was reflecting upon the rest (of the things) that are exalted, Jesus said to him, "Step away from

---

18. Here Jesus indicates that the anger rising within the hearts of the disciples is being provoked by their God within them. Jesus challenges them to allow the true person—the spiritual person—to come to expression and stand before him.
19. Here and elsewhere in the text, "spirit" apparently means living being. See Gospel of Judas 43, 53.
20. Of the disciples, only Judas has the strength to stand before Jesus, and he does so with modesty and respect. On Judas averting his eyes before Jesus, see Gospel of Thomas 46, where it is said that people should show a similar form of modesty by lowering the eyes before John the Baptizer.
21. Or, "eternal realm," here and below.
22. In the Gospel of Judas, it is Judas himself who provides the true confession of who Jesus is. To confess that Jesus is from the immortal aeon (or eternal realm) of Barbelo is to profess, in Sethian terms, that Jesus is from the divine realm above and is the son of God. In Sethian texts, Barbelo may be presented as the divine Mother of all, who often is said to be the Forethought (*pronoia*) of the Father, the infinite One. The name of Barbelo seems to be based on a form of the tetragrammaton, the holy four-letter name of God within Judaism, and it apparently comes from Hebrew (perhaps "God (compare *El*) in (*b*-) four (*arb*(*a*)"). For presentations of Barbelo in Sethian literature, see Secret Book of John II:4-5; Holy Book of the Great Invisible Spirit (also known as the Egyptian Gospel; Nag Hammadi Codex III), 42, 62, 69; Zostrianos 14, 124, 129; Allogenes the Stranger 51, 53, 56; and Three Forms of First Thought 38.
23. The one who has sent Jesus is the ineffable God. The ineffability of the divine is also asserted in Gospel of Judas 47, and it is emphasized in such Sethian texts as

the others and I shall tell you the mysteries of the kingdom,[24] not so that you will go there,[25] but you[26] will grieve
a great deal. [*36*] For someone else will replace you, in order
that the twelve [disciples] may again come to completion
with their God."[27]

And Judas said to him, "When will you tell me these
things, and (when) will the great day of light dawn for the
[. . .] generation?"[28]

But when he said this, Jesus left him.[29]

JESUS APPEARS TO THE DISCIPLES AGAIN

Now, the next morning, after this happened,[30] he appeared to
his disciples (again).

And they said to him, "Master, where did you go and what
did you do when you left us?"

Jesus said to them, "I went to another great and holy
generation."[31]

---

the Secret Book of John, the Holy Book of the Great Invisible Spirit, and Allogenes the Stranger. In Gospel of Thomas 13, Thomas similarly declares to Jesus,
"Teacher, my mouth is utterly unable to say what you are like."

24. Or, "reign"—that is, the kingdom or reign of God.

25. This translation is based on the Coptic *oukh hina je ekebōk emau*. The ink traces
on the papyrus remain faint and difficult to read. In the first edition of *The
Gospel of Judas*, we translated this "It is possible for you to reach it," based on
the transcription *oun com je ekebōk emau*, a reading Gesine Schenke Robinson
still prefers.

26. Or, "that you."

27. See Acts 1:15-26 on the selection of Matthias to replace Judas in the circle of
the twelve.

28. The ink traces are very uncertain here. We expect a relative complement to *genea*,
"generation," but the traces do not seem to fit either *etjoor*, "strong," or *etouaab*,
"holy," just below.

29. Judas asks questions about the promised revelation from Jesus and the ultimate
glorification of that generation, but Jesus abruptly leaves.

30. Or, "At dawn of the next day."

31. Jesus maintains that he went beyond this world to another realm, apparently the
spiritual realm of that generation.

His disciples said to him, "Lord, what is the great generation that is superior to us and holy, that is not now in these aeons?"[32]

When Jesus heard this, he laughed. He said to them, "Why are you thinking in your hearts about the strong and holy generation? [*37*] Truly[33] [I] say to you, no one born [of] this aeon will see that [generation], and no host of angels of the stars will rule over that generation, and no person of mortal birth will be able to associate with it, because that generation is not from [. . .] that has come into being, [but . . . the] generation of people among [you] is from the generation of humanity[34] [. . .] power, which [. . .] powers [. . . by] which you rule."

When [his] disciples heard this, they each were troubled in [their] spirit. They did not find a word to say.

THE DISCIPLES BEHOLD THE TEMPLE AND DISCUSS IT

Another day Jesus came up to [them]. They said to [him], "Master, we have seen you in a [vision], for we have had great [dreams during this] night that has passed."

[He said], "Why have [you . . . and] gone into hiding?" [*38*]

And they[35] [said, "We have] seen a great house [with a] large altar [in it, and] twelve men—they are the priests, we

---

32. These realms or aeons are the ones, here below, that are mere copies or reflections of the realms or aeons above. This theme is discussed more fully later in the text. The Platonic character of this theme is clear, but the Platonic concept of the realm of ideas and the reflections of ideas in our world is interpreted in a gnostic manner in the Gospel of Judas and other texts, especially Sethian texts.

33. Amen.

34. In this passage, Jesus seems to say that the great generation comes from above and is indomitable and that people who are part of this world below live in mortality and cannot attain that great generation.

35. This section of the text suggests that the disciples have a vision of the Jewish temple in Jerusalem—or, less likely, that they have gone to visit the temple—and then they report on what they have seen. (Note the pronouns in the first-person plural "we" in this passage.) See the accounts in the New Testament gospels of the visits of Jesus and the disciples to the temple: Matthew 21:12-17 and 24:1-25:46; Mark 11:15-19 and 13:1-37; Luke 19:45-48 and 21:5-38; and John 2:13-22.

would say; and a name < . . . >;[36] and a crowd of people is waiting at that altar,[37] [until] the priests [finished presenting] the offerings. We [also] kept waiting."

[Jesus said], "What are [. . .] like?"[38]

And they [said], "Some [. . . for][39] two weeks; [others] sacrifice their own children, others their wives, in praise [and] in humility with each other; others sleep with men; others are involved in slaugh[ter]; still others commit a multitude of sins and deeds of lawlessness. [And] the men who stand [before] the altar invoke your [name]. [*39*] And while they are involved in all the deeds of their sacrifice,[40] that [altar] is filled."

After they said this, they were quiet, for they were troubled.

JESUS OFFERS AN ALLEGORICAL INTERPRETATION OF THE VISION OF THE TEMPLE

Jesus said to them, "Why are you troubled? Truly[41] I say to you, all the priests who stand before that altar invoke my

---

36. Perhaps the name of Jesus; see Gospel of Judas 38 ("your [name]") and 39 ("my name"). In the context of the Jewish temple in Jerusalem, the reference to "a name" could also be understood to refer to the ineffable name of God (Yahweh) within Judaism. As Wolf-Peter Funk suggests, it is possible that "and a name (*auō ouran*) is the beginning of a new sentence, and something has been omitted by the scribe, so that the sentence may be thought to have read "and a name <was invoked/was written on . . . >," or the like.

37. Here the text seems inadvertently to repeat "at the altar" (a case of dittography).

38. Here probably restore to read "[the priests]," or else "[the crowd]", "[the people]" (as suggested by Peter Nagel).

39. Probably restore to read "[abstain for]"; see Gospel of Judas 40.

40. The Coptic word *šōōt* may be translated as either "sacrifice" or "deficiency." With the former translation, the passage continues to focus attention upon the issue of sacrifice in the text. With the latter translation, the passage employs a technical word in Sethian and other texts for the lack of divine light and knowledge that can be traced to the fall of the mother—usually Sophia, the Wisdom of God—and the subsequent loss of enlightenment. See, for example, Letter of Peter to Philip 3-4 (Codex Tchacos) and 135 (Nag Hammadi Codex VIII), quoted on pages 134-135 below. On corruptible wisdom, see Gospel of Judas 44.

41. Amen.

name. And again I say to you, my name has been written on [. . .] of the generations of the stars by the human generations. [And] they have planted trees without fruit, in my name, in a shameful manner."[42]

Jesus said to them, "It is you who are presenting the offerings on the altar you have seen.[43] That one is the God you serve, and you are the twelve men you have seen. And the cattle that are brought in are the sacrifices you have seen—that is, the many people you lead astray [*40*] before that altar. [The . . .][44] will stand up and make use of my name in this way, and <the> generations of the pious will be loyal to him. After him[45] another man will stand up from[46] the [fornicators], and another [will] stand up from the slayers of children,[47] and another from those who sleep[48] with men and those who

---

42. The reference to planting trees without fruit, in the name of Jesus, seems to be an indictment of those who preach in the name of Jesus but proclaim a gospel without fruitful content. The same image of trees bearing or not bearing fruit is found in Revelation of Adam 76, 85. See Gospel of Judas 43. Also compare, perhaps, the withered fig tree of Matthew 21:18-19 and Mark 11:12-14.

43. Throughout this section Jesus interprets what the disciples have seen at the temple as a metaphor for erroneous religious practice, specifically sacrifice, apparently in the emerging orthodox church. The priests are the disciples, and apparently their successors in the church, and the animals led to the slaughter are the victims of the improper religious observance in the church.

44. Perhaps restore to read "[The . . . overseer (or, bishop)]," or "[The minister (or, deacon)]," or possibly "[The ruler (or, archon) of this world]"; see 1 Corinthians 2:8.

45. Or, "After that."

46. Coptic, from Greek, *parista* (two lines later, *parhista*). The people who stand up appear to be leaders in the emerging orthodox church who are judged, in this polemical section, to be working as assistants of the God of this world. The verb may also be translated "represent," here and below, rather than "stand up from."

47. Here the text seems to suggest that the leaders of the emerging orthodox church are immoral in their own lives and are endangering the lives of the children of God by emphasizing sacrificial themes and leading the people into spiritual death or, according to Elaine Pagels and Karen L. King, martyrdom. This image may recall the comparison with cattle being led to death in temple sacrifice.

48. Or, "have sex." Here we read *nrefnkotke* for *nrefnkokte* of the manuscript. The accusation of sexual impropriety is a standard feature of polemical argumentation. One's opponents are frequently said to be immoral people.

abstain,[49] and the rest of the people of pollution and law-lessness and error, and those who say, 'We are like angels';[50] they are the stars that bring everything to completion. For to the human generations it has been said, 'Look, God has received your sacrifice from the hands of priests,'[51] that is, a minister of error. But the Lord, who commands, is he who is the Lord of the universe.[52] On the last day they will be put to shame."[53] [*41*]

Jesus said [to them], "Stop sac[rificing . . .] which you have [. . .] over the altar, since they are over your stars and your angels and have already come to their conclusion there.[54] So let them be [. . .][55] before you, and let them go [—*about 15 lines missing*—][56] generations [. . .]. A baker cannot feed all creation [*42*] under [heaven]."[57]

And [when the disciples heard] th[ese (words)], they said to him, "Lord, help us and save us."[58]

---

49. Literally, "fast." For a similar negative view of fasting, see Gospel of Thomas 6.
50. Here the text inadvertently has the word "and."
51. Perhaps read, instead, "a priest," in order for there to be agreement with "a minister."
52. Or, "All"—that is, the fullness of the divine realm above (Coptic *ptērf*).
53. At the end of time, the leaders of the emerging orthodox church will be punished for their acts of impiety.
54. Here Jesus seems to indicate that the leaders of the emerging orthodox church are strong, but their time is coming to an end.
55. Perhaps read "[entrapped]" or "[upbraided]." The reading and meaning of the text are uncertain. The Coptic (possibly *šōnt*, literally "entwined") may also be translated "quarreling" or "in a struggle."
56. An extant photograph from an earlier inspection of the codex, though lacking in clarity, reveals a few words and expressions.
57. This statement may be an ancient proverb about setting reasonable goals for what people can accomplish—in this case, readers of the Gospel of Judas who face the opposition of the emerging orthodox church. Conversely, the statement may also be intended as a critique of the Eucharist as it is celebrated in the emerging orthodox church.
58. Restored, since the publication of the critical edition, by Wolf-Peter Funk and Gesine Schenke Robinson.

Jesus said to them, "Stop struggling with me. Each of you has his own star,[59] [and every]one [—*about 17 lines missing*—] [*43*] in [. . .] who[60] has not come [. . . spring] for the tree[61] [. . .] of this aeon[62] [. . .] after a time [. . .] but he[63] has come to water God's paradise,[64] and the race[65] that will last, because [he] will not defile the [walk of life of] that generation, but [. . .] for all eternity."[66]

JUDAS ASKS JESUS ABOUT THAT GENERATION
Judas said to [him, "Rabb]i (?),[67] what kind of fruit does this generation produce?"[68]

Jesus said, "The souls of every human generation will die. When these people, however, have completed the time of the kingdom and the spirit[69] leaves them, their bodies will die, but their souls will be alive, and they will be taken up."

---

59. The teaching here and elsewhere in the Gospel of Judas that each person has a star seems to reflect Plato's presentation in his *Timaeus* and other Platonic texts. After citing a statement by the creator of the world, it is said there that the creator "assigned each soul to a star" and declared that "the person who lived well during his appointed time was to return and dwell in his native star" (41d-42b; quoted below on page 144-145). On the star of Judas, see Gospel of Judas 57. April DeConick has argued that, throughout the Gospel of Judas, the stars are a negative part of the world below.
60. Or, "which."
61. The reference to a tree, in this fragmentary portion of the text, may indicate one of the trees in paradise. The trees of the garden of Eden are frequently discussed in gnostic texts, and the tree of the knowledge (Greek *gnōsis*) of good and evil is often thought to be a source of the knowledge of God. See Secret Book of John II:22-23.
62. Perhaps restore to read "[ti]me of this aeon," as suggested by Pierre Cherix, Peter Nagel, and John D. Turner.
63. Or, "it." The identity of the pronominal subject here and in the next lines is uncertain.
64. See Genesis 2:10.
65. Or, perhaps, "generation." Here and elsewhere in text, rather than the Coptic *genea*, "generation," which is usually employed, the Coptic reads *genos*. Both words derive from Greek.
66. Literally, "from everlasting to everlasting."
67. The title "rabbi" (largely restored) is the Hebrew term for a Jewish teacher or master.
68. Compare and contrast Gospel of Judas 39 on those who plant trees without fruit.
69. The spirit or breath of life? On spirit and soul, see also Gospel of Judas 53.

Judas said, "And what will the rest of the human generations do?"

Jesus said, "It is impossible [**44**] to sow seed on [rock] and
harvest its fruit.[70] This is also the way [. . .] of the [defiled] race[71]
and corruptible wisdom[72] [. . .] the hand that has created mortal people, and their souls go up to the aeons on high. [Truly][73]
I say to you, [no authority][74] or angel [or] power will be able to
see those [realms] that [this great], holy generation [will see]."

After Jesus said this, he departed.[75]

JUDAS RECOUNTS A VISION AND JESUS RESPONDS

Judas said, "Master, as you have listened to all of them, now
also listen to me. For I have seen a great vision."

When Jesus heard this, he laughed and said to him, "You
thirteenth daimon,[76] why do you try so hard? But speak up,
and I shall bear with you."

---

70. See the parable of the sower in Matthew 13:1-23, Mark 4:1-20, Luke 8:4-15, and
Gospel of Thomas 9. According to the parable, seed that is sown on rock cannot
take root and thus cannot produce heads of grain.

71. Or, perhaps, "generation," as above.

72. Or, "Wisdom," "Sophia," the personified figure of Wisdom, who is that part of
the divine, in gnostic tradition, that falls through a lapse of wisdom and is eventually restored to the fullness of the divine once again. Wisdom is mentioned
only here on the extant pages of the Gospel of Judas. Sophia is often personified
as a female figure in Jewish and Christian literature, and she plays a central role
in many gnostic texts, including Sethian texts. See, for example, the account of
the fall of Sophia in Secret Book of John II:9-10, quoted below on page 134. The
child of Sophia, according to gnostic accounts, is the demiurge Saklas or Yaldabaoth. See Gospel of Judas 51. The figure of Judas may be presented in the Gospel
of Judas in such a way as to recall Sophia in the Pistis Sophia and the comments
of Irenaeus of Lyon about Judas as a type and image of Sophia among second-
century Valentinian gnostics. See commentary, pages 146-152.

73. Amen.

74. Or, "[no man]," as proposed by Wolf-Peter Funk.

75. Perhaps emend to read "<they> departed."

76. Or, "thirteenth demon," "thirteenth spirit" (Coptic, from Greek, *daimōn*). Judas
may be understood to be the thirteenth because he is the disciple excluded from
the circle of the twelve, and he is linked to the thirteenth aeon in the Gospel of

Judas said to him, "In the vision I saw the twelve disciples stoning me and [*45*] persecuting [me severely]. And I also
came to the place where [. . .] after you. I saw [a house . . .],[77]
and my eyes could not [comprehend] its size. And great
people were surrounding it, and that house <had> a single
room,[78] and in the middle of the house was [a crowd—*nearly*
two lines missing—], (saying), 'Master, take me in along with
these people.'"

[Jesus] answered and said, "Your star has led you astray,
Judas." And (he continued), "No person of mortal birth is worthy to enter the house you have seen, for that place is reserved
for the holy.[79] Neither the sun nor the moon will rule there,
nor the day, but the holy will abide[80] always in the aeon with
the holy angels.[81] Look, I have explained to you the mysteries

---

Judas in a way that recalls Sophia's connections with the thirteenth aeon in the
Pistis Sophia. Sometimes in Sethian thought the thirteenth aeon is also considered the dwelling place of the ruler of this world. The word *daimōn* can mean
"demon" in a thoroughly negative sense of the term, as in Jewish and Christian
literature; the words *daimōn* and *daimonion* can also be used in a more neutral
or even positive sense, in Platonic, Middle Platonic, Neoplatonic, Hermetic, and
magical texts, where *daimones* commonly are thought to be intermediary beings
that find their place between the divine and human realms. Compare tales of
Socrates and his *daimōn* or *daimonion* in Plato (*Apology*; see also the *Symposium*).
In a manner that resembles the present passage in the Gospel of Judas, Sophia is
made to liken herself to a *daimōn* in this mortal world in the Pistis Sophia.

77. Judas reports a vision in which he is harshly opposed by the other disciples (see
Gospel of Judas 35-36, 46-47). In the vision Judas approaches a place and makes
mention of Jesus ("after you"); there is a great heavenly house there, and Judas
asks that he may be received into that great house along with the others who are
entering. On the heavenly house or mansion, see John 14:1-14.

78. Or, "a single roof." The translation above follows Jacques van der Vliet's reading.
Previous suggestions included "roof of greenery" and "<broad> roof."

79. Or, "the saints," here and below.

80. Or, "stand."

81. On this apocalyptic description of heaven, see Revelation 21:23. According to
Secret Book of John II:9, the souls of the holy or the saints dwell in the third
eternal realm, with the third luminary Daveithai, the home of the offspring of
Seth. See also Holy Book of the Great Invisible Spirit III:50-51.

of the kingdom [*46*] and I have taught you about the error of the stars; and [. . .] send [. . .] on the twelve aeons."

JUDAS ASKS ABOUT HIS OWN FATE

Judas said, "Master, could it be that my seed[82] is under the control of the rulers?"[83]

Jesus answered and said to him, "Come, that I [*—about two lines missing—*], but you[84] will grieve much when you see the kingdom and all its generation."

When Judas heard this, he said to him, "What is the advantage that I have received? For you have set me apart from that generation."[85]

Jesus answered and said, "You will become the thirteenth,[86] and you will be cursed by the other generations, and you will come to rule over them.[87] In the last days they <will . . . > to you, and you[88] will not ascend on high[89] [*47*] to the holy [generation]."

---

82. The seed is the spiritual part of a person, the spark of the divine within, and, collectively, the offspring of those who come from the divine. Thus, in Sethian texts gnostics can be called the seed or offspring of Seth.

83. Or, "archons," here and below—that is, the rulers of this world, especially the cosmic powers who collaborate with the demiurge. This clause may also be translated "that my seed subdues the rulers?"

84. Or, "that you."

85. Previously, this phrase was translated "for that generation," with the current translation as the alternate. On "What is the advantage," compare Genesis 37:26, on Judah (Greek, Judas), following Louis Painchaud's suggestion.

86. On Judas as the thirteenth, see Gospel of Judas 44, where Judas is said to be the thirteenth daimon. See also the discussion below, pages 146-152.

87. On Judas being cursed, compare the assessments of Judas in Matthew 26:20-25 and 27:3-10; Mark 14:17-21; Luke 22:21-23; John 13:21-30; and Acts 1:15-20. Here it is suggested that Judas is despised by the other disciples, but he is to be exalted over them (and the rulers of this world).

88. Or, perhaps, "that you."

89. These lines remain difficult to read and interpret. It may well be that some letters or words have dropped out, as Wolf-Peter Funk and Peter Nagel suggest. In an earlier examination of the Coptic text, we suggested that these lines could be read

JESUS TEACHES JUDAS ABOUT COSMOLOGY

Jesus said, "[Come], that I may teach you about the [(things) . . .][90] that [no (?)] human will (ever) see. For there exists a great and boundless aeon, whose extent no generation of angels could (?) see, [in] which is the great invisible Spirit,[91]

> *which no eye of an [angel] has ever seen,*
>
> *no thought of the heart has ever comprehended,*
>
> *and it was never called by any name.*[92]

---

without assuming that there had been a mistake made in the textual tradition, and we translated the passage in the first edition of *The Gospel of Judas*, tentatively and with difficulty, as follows: "In the last days they will (*sena-*) curse (*kauō*) your (*nek-*) ascent (*ktē epšōi*, as the object of the verb) to the holy [generation]." (The ink traces we once read as *ktē* are very faint.) The present translation assumes that *se<na-* . . . >, "they <will . . . >," is the opening of an incomplete verb in the future tense; that *nak*, "to you," is a prepositional phrase; that *auō*, "and," is a conjunction; that *nek*, "you will not," indicates a negative third future form of a verb; and that *bōk epšōi*, "ascend on high," is a verb (with *bōk*, a new reading of the ink traces). Other reconstructions may also be possible.

90. The restoration is uncertain, but the definite article is plural. For a full account of Sethian cosmology, see the Secret Book of John; see also the Holy Book of the Great Invisible Spirit.

91. In many Sethian texts—for example, the Secret Book of John and the Holy Book of the Great Invisible Spirit—the transcendent deity is called the great invisible Spirit.

92. See 1 Corinthians 2:9, Gospel of Thomas 17, Prayer of the Apostle Paul A, etc. The parallel text in the Valentinian Prayer of the Apostle Paul is close to part of the formulation in the Gospel of Judas: "Grant what eyes of angels have not [seen], what ears of rulers have not heard, and what has not arisen in the human heart, which became angelic, made in the image of the animate God when it was formed in the beginning." The ineffability and transcendence of the divine is emphasized in many gnostic texts, especially Sethian texts. See Secret Book of John II:2-4, Holy Book of the Great Invisible Spirit III:40-41, and Allogenes the Stranger; also see Irenaeus of Lyon, *Against Heresies* 1.29.1-4, on the "gnostics" or "Barbelognostics" ("gnostics of Barbelo"); and Gospel of Judas 35. Lines from the Secret Book of John illustrating such descriptions of divine transcendence are quoted below on pages 129-130.

"And a luminous cloud[93] appeared there. And he[94] said,
'Let an angel[95] come into being as my attendant.'[96]

"And a great angel, the Self-Generated,[97] the God of the
light, emerged from the cloud. And because of him, four other
angels came into being from another cloud, and they became
attendants[98] for the angelic Self-Generated.[99] And [**48**] the
Self-Generated said, 'Let A[damas][100] come into being,' and
[the emanation][101] occurred. And he [created] the first luminary[102] for [him] to reign over. And he said, 'Let angels come
into being to serve [him,'[103] and myriads] without number
came into being. And he said, '[Let] a luminous aeon come
into being,' and he[104] came into being. He created the second

---

93. Or, "cloud of light." The luminous cloud is a manifestation of the glorious heavenly
presence of the divine, and clouds of light often appear in ancient descriptions of
theophanies. In the accounts of the transfiguration of Jesus in the New Testament
gospels, for instance, luminous clouds accompany the revelation of glory (Matthew
17:5-6, Mark 9:7-8, and Luke 9:34-35). In the Holy Book of the Great Invisible
Spirit heavenly clouds also play an important role; in the Secret Book of John there
is light surrounding the Father of All.

94. The Spirit.

95. Or, "messenger," here and below.

96. Or, "as my assistant," "for my assistance," "to stand by me" (Coptic, from Greek,
parastasis), here and below. Compare the verb *parista/parhista* in Gospel of Judas 40.

97. Or, "Self-Begotten," "Self-Engendered," "Self-Conceived," "Autogenes" (Coptic
autogenēs, from Greek), here and below. Typically, the Self-Generated is the child
of God in Sethian texts; see Secret Book of John II:7-9; Holy Book of the Great
Invisible Spirit III:49 and IV:60; Zostrianos 6, 7, and 127; and Allogenes the
Stranger 46, 51, and 58.

98. Again, Coptic, from Greek, *parastasis.*

99. In Secret Book of John II:7-8, the Four Luminaries, named Harmozel, Oroiael,
Daveithai, and Eleleth, come into being through the Self-Generated. See Holy
Book of the Great Invisible Spirit III:51-53, Zostrianos 127-28, and Three Forms
of First Thought 38-39.

100. Restored by Uwe-Karsten Plisch. On Adamas, see note 106 below.

101. Restored by John D. Turner.

102. Coptic, from Greek, *phōstēr*, here and below.

103. Or, "offer adoration [to him]," "offer worship [to him]" (Coptic *šmše*, here and
below).

104. Or, "it," in reference to the aeon, here and below.

luminary [to] reign over him, together with myriads of angels without number, to offer service. And that is how he created the rest of the aeons of the light. And he made them reign over them, and he created for them myriads of angels without number, to assist them. [105]

ADAMAS AND THE LUMINARIES

"Adamas[106] was in the first cloud of light[107] that no angel could (?) (ever) see among all those called 'divine.' And he [**49**] [. . .] that [. . . after] the image [of . . .] and after the likeness of [this] angel.[108] He made the incorruptible [generation] of Seth[109] appear to the twelve l[uminaries],[110] the 24 [. . .]. He made 72 luminaries appear in the incorruptible generation, in accordance with the will of the Spirit. And the 72 luminaries themselves made 360 luminaries appear in the incorruptible generation, in accordance with the will of the Spirit, that their number should be five for each. [111]

"And the twelve aeons of the twelve luminaries constitute their Father, with six heavens for each aeon, so that there are

---

105. According to the text, the divine realm is filled with luminaries, aeons, and angels brought into being by the creative word of the Self-Generated, to serve and adore the divine.

106. Adamas is Adam, the first human of Genesis, here understood, as in many other gnostic texts, as the paradigmatic human of the divine realm and the exalted image of humanity. See, for example, Secret Book of John II:8-9.

107. The first luminous cloud is the initial manifestation of the divine; see Gospel of Judas 47.

108. Or, "of [these] angels," as suggested by John D. Turner.

109. This is Seth son of Adam, also in the divine realm. See Genesis 4:25–5:8. The role of Seth as the progenitor of the generation of Seth ("that generation") is well established in Sethian texts. See also Gospel of Judas 52.

110. The reading "l[uminaries]" (partially restored) is based on a fragment placed since the publication of the critical edition, but the sentence remains difficult. Such a restoration as "the twelve l[uminaries in] the 24 [. . .]" or "the twelve l[uminaries of] the 24 [. . .]" could be imagined, but the amount of space available at the end of the line may not allow for such possibilities.

111. Everything finally happens in accordance with the will of the divine, the Spirit.

72 heavens for the 72 luminaries, and for each [**50**] [of them five] firmaments, [for a total of] 360 [firmaments. They] were given authority and a [great] host of angels without number, for glory and adoration, and also virgin[112] spirits,[113] for glory and [adoration] of all the aeons and the heavens and their firmaments.[114]

THE COSMOS, CHAOS, AND THE UNDERWORLD

"Now, the multitude of those immortals is called 'cosmos'— that is, corruption[115]—by the Father and the 72 luminaries who are with the Self-Generated and his 72 aeons. In that place[116] the first human appeared with his incorruptible powers. And the aeon that appeared with his generation, the one in whom are the cloud of knowledge[117] and the angel, is called [**51**]

---

112. In Sethian texts, the term *virgin* is used as an epithet for a variety of divine manifestations and powers to stress their purity. In the Holy Book of the Great Invisible Spirit, for example, the great invisible Spirit, Barbelo, Youel, and Plesithea are described as virgins, and additional mention is made of more virgins.

113. Eugnostos the Blessed includes a passage on the aeons that also mentions virgin spirits, and this passage (Nag Hammadi Codex III:88-89, cited in the commentary below, page 133) is very close to the text under consideration. See also Wisdom of Jesus Christ (Nag Hammadi Codex III) 113 and On the Origin of the World 105-6.

114. These aeons and luminaries, the spiritual powers of the universe, represent aspects of the world, especially time and units of time. On the twelve aeons, compare the months of the year. On the 72 heavens and luminaries, compare the traditional number of nations in the world according to Jewish lore. On the 360 firmaments, compare the number of days in the solar year (30 days per month, for twelve months), without five intercalary days. This passage in the Gospel of Judas is paralleled in Eugnostos the Blessed III:83-84 (cited in the commentary below, page 132-133), and in the lines that follow in Eugnostos the Blessed, the author discusses the similar number of aeons, heavens, and firmaments.

115. Our cosmos, unlike the divine realm above, is susceptible to decay and hence may be termed a realm of corruption.

116. Or, "There."

117. Coptic, from Greek, *gnōsis*.

El (?)[118] [—*portions of two lines missing*—] aeon [. . .]. After that [. . .] said, 'Let twelve angels come into being [to] rule over chaos and the [underworld].' And look, from the cloud there appeared an [angel] whose face flashed with fire and whose appearance was defiled with blood. His name was Nebro,[119] which means in translation 'rebel';[120] others call him Yaldabaoth.[121] And another angel, Saklas,[122] also came from the cloud. So Nebro created six angels, as well as Saklas, to be assistants, and these produced twelve angels in the heavens, with each one receiving a portion in the heavens.[123]

---

118. El is an ancient Semitic name for God. In Sethian texts related names, such as Eloaios, are used for powers and authorities of this world. The Secret Book of John also refers to Elohim, the Hebrew word for God in the Jewish Scriptures. Here John D. Turner and April DeConick prefer the reading "El[eleth]"; see the role of Eleleth in the Secret Book of John, the Holy Book of the Great Invisible Spirit, and the Three Forms of First Thought. Gregor Wurst observes, however, that the supralinear stroke over El seems to end with the "l," and the ink traces that follow do not fit well with "Eleleth." Elsewhere in the Gospel of Judas and Codex Tchacos, names of heavenly beings may be given without honorific or expanded endings (for instance, Nebro rather than Nebroel or Nebruel in the Gospel of Judas and Addon rather than Ad(d)onaios in James).

119. In the Holy Book of the Great Invisible Spirit III:57, Nebruel is a great demoness who mates with Sakla and produces twelve aeons; note the role of Nebroel in Manichaean texts. Here the name Nebro is given without the honorific suffix -el (also "God" in Hebrew). In Secret Book of John II:10, the demiurge Yaldabaoth has the appearance of a snake with the face of a lion, and his eyes are like flashing bolts of lightning. In Holy Book of the Great Invisible Spirit III:56-57, Sophia of matter is bloody in appearance: "A cloud [named] Sophia of matter appeared . . . . [She] surveyed the regions [of chaos], and her face looked like . . . in her appearance . . . blood."

120. Or, "apostate" (Coptic, from Greek, *apostatēs*). Nebro likely derives from Nebrod in Genesis 10:8-12 (see 1 Chronicles 1:10) of the Septuagint (Hebrew Nimrod, possibly meaning "rebel"). Louis Painchaud sees "apostate" as part of a warning against gnostic apostasy.

121. Yaldabaoth is a common name for the demiurge in Sethian texts. Yaldabaoth may mean "child of chaos" (or "child of (S)abaoth") in Aramaic.

122. Saklas (or Sakla, as in Gospel of Judas 52) is another common name for the demiurge in Sethian texts. Saklas (or Sakla) means "fool" in Aramaic.

123. The syntax of this sentence is not entirely clear, so that the role of Saklas and his relationship with Nebro remain uncertain. If Nebro and Saklas each create six angels, that accounts for the twelve angels that are produced. See Holy Book of the Great Invisible

THE RULERS AND ANGELS

"And the twelve rulers spoke with the twelve angels: 'Let each of you [*52*] [. . .] and let them [. . .] generation [. . . five][124] angels':

The first is [(?)e]th, who is called 'the Christ.'[125]

The [second] is Harmathoth, who is [. . .].[126]

The [third] is Galila.

The fourth is Yobel.

The fifth is Adonaios.

"These are the five who ruled over the underworld, and first of all[127] over chaos.[128]

Spirit III:57-58: "Sakla the great [angel observed] Nebruel the great demon who is with him. [Together] they brought a spirit of reproduction to the earth, and [they produced] angelic assistants. Sakla [said] to Nebruel the great [demon], 'Let twelve realms come into being in the . . . realm, worlds . . . .' Through the will of the Self-Generated, [Sakla] the great angel said, 'There shall be . . . seven in number. . . .'" The twelve angelic portions in the heavens may designate the twelve signs of the zodiac.

124. Restored by Peter Nagel.

125. Or, "[Se]th." As in other Sethian texts, Christ may be described as the manifestation of Seth in this world, although the placement of these names in this cosmological context is peculiar. In Holy Book of the Great Invisible Spirit III:63-64, the text refers to "the incorruptible one, conceived by the Word (Logos), the living Jesus, with whom great Seth has been clothed." In Three Forms of First Thought 50, the Word, or Logos, declares, "I put on Jesus. I carried him from the accursed wood (the cross) and established him in the dwelling places of his Father." See Gospel of Judas 56. Rather than "[Se]th, who is called 'the Christ (*kh*(*risto*)*s*),'" John D. Turner and April DeConick prefer "[Ath]eth, who is called 'the good one' (reading *kh*(*rēsto*)*s*)," and Jacques van der Vliet suggests the reading "[Se]th, who is called Aries (the Ram, Greek *krios*, wrongly taken by a copyist as *kh*(*risto*)*s*)."

126. Here April DeConick reads "Harmathoth, who is [the evil eye]," after John D. Turner; see Secret Book of John II:10.

127. Or, "and the first ones," following Jacques van der Vliet's reading. This translation may assume that the names of the first angels have been omitted from the text. See the parallel passages in the Holy Book of the Great Invisible Spirit and the Secret Book of John.

128. In Holy Book of the Great Invisible Spirit III:58, through Nebruel and Sakla twelve angels are produced, and several of the names are similar or identical

THE CREATION OF HUMANITY

"Then Saklas said to his angels, 'Let us create a human being after the likeness and after the image.'[129] And they fashioned Adam and his wife Eve. But she is called, in the cloud, 'Zoe.'[130] For by this name all the generations seek him (Adam), and each of them calls her (Eve) by their names. Now, Sakla did not [53] com[mand . . .] except [. . .] the gene[rations . . .] this [. . .]. And the [ruler] said to him, 'Your life will last [for a . . .] time,[131] with your children.'"

JUDAS ASKS ABOUT THE DESTINY OF ADAM AND HUMANITY

And Judas said to Jesus, "[What] is the advantage of human life?"[132]

Jesus said, "Why are you wondering about this, that Adam, with his generation, has received his span of life in such a number in the place where he has received his kingdom in such a number with his ruler?"[133]

---

to the names here. In Secret Book of John II:10-11, a similar list of names is given, and it is said that seven rule over the seven spheres of heaven (for the sun, moon, and five planets—Mercury, Venus, Mars, Jupiter, and Saturn) and five rule over the depth of the abyss. In the Gospel of Judas, the unusual name Harmathoth appears to be a conflation of Harmas and Athoth, perhaps to accommodate the reference to Seth.

129. See Genesis 1:26. Similar accounts of the creation of a human being are found in other Sethian texts, and sometimes it is said, in more fully developed traditions, that the human is created after the image of God above and with a likeness to the rulers of this world. See also Secret Book of John II:14-15, cited below on page 143.

130. Zoe, Greek for "life," is the name of Eve in the Septuagint.

131. This phrase may be restored to read "[for a long] time," "[for you] for a time" (Peter Nagel), or "[for a short] time" (Louis Painchaud).

132. On the translation, compare, with Louis Painchaud, Ecclesiastes 6:11-12.

133. This sentence is difficult and the translation tentative, but it seems to mean that Judas is wondering about Adam in his world with his length of life and his God—all of which is irrelevant for Judas. John D. Turner suggests that it may mean the following: "Why are you wondering about this, that Adam, with his generation, has received his limited span of life in the place where he has

Judas said to Jesus, "Does the human spirit die?"

Jesus said, "In this way God ordered Michael to give the spirits of people to them as a loan, so that they might offer service. But the Great One ordered Gabriel[134] to grant spirits to the great generation with no ruler over it[135]—the spirit and the soul.[136] Therefore, the [rest] of the souls [*54*] [. . .].

JESUS DISCUSSES THE DESTRUCTION
OF THE WICKED WITH JUDAS AND OTHERS

"[. . .] light [. . .] chaos [. . .] surround [. . .] spirit within you,[137] [which] you have let dwell in this [flesh] (coming) from the generations of angels. But God caused knowledge[138] to be [given][139] to Adam and those with him,[140] so that the kings of chaos and the underworld might not lord it over them."

---

received his limited kingdom with his ruler?" At the end, the text may inadvertently repeat the phrase "in such a number" (dittography).

134. Michael and Gabriel are two prominent archangels.

135. Or, "the kingless generation," a reference to the generation of Seth, using a description familiar from Sethian texts to indicate that the people of Seth are indomitable.

136. God (the God of this world?) gives the spirit of life (the breath of life? see, perhaps, Genesis 2:7) to people, through Michael, as a loan, but the Great Spirit gives spirit and soul to people, through Gabriel, as a gift. Genesis 2:7 can be interpreted creatively in other gnostic texts, including Sethian texts; see Secret Book of John II:19: "They (five luminaries from above) said to Yaldabaoth, 'Breathe some of your spirit into the face of Adam, and the body will arise.' He breathed his spirit into Adam. The spirit is the power of his mother (Sophia), but he did not realize this, because he lives in ignorance. The Mother's power went out of Yaldabaoth and into the psychical body that had been made to be like the one who is from the beginning. The body moved, and became powerful. And it was enlightened." On spirit and soul in the present text, see also Gospel of Judas 43.

137. Plural.

138. Again, Coptic, from Greek, *gnōsis*.

139. Or, "[brought]."

140. This passage suggests that *gnōsis*, or knowledge, is given to Adam and thus to humanity. The way in which Adam and humanity come to possess knowledge is explained in detail in other gnostic texts, including Sethian texts, and in these

[And] Judas said to Jesus, "So what will those generations do?"

Jesus said, "Truly[141] I say to you,[142] above them all, the stars bring matters to completion.[143] And when Saklas completes the span of time assigned for him, their first star will appear with the generations, and they will finish what has been said (above). Then they will fornicate in my name and slay their children[144] [**55**] and [they will . . .][145] and [—*about six and a half lines missing*—in] my name, and your star will ru[le] over the [thir]teenth aeon."[146]

And after that Jesus [laughed].

[Judas said], "Master, [why are you laughing at us]?"[147]

[Jesus] answered [and said], "I am not laughing [at] you but at the error of the stars, because these six stars wander about with these five combatants, and they all will be destroyed along with their creatures."[148]

---

texts it is asserted that humanity has knowledge but the megalomaniacal rulers of this world do not.

141. Here and below, the Coptic word *alēthōs* (from Greek) is used rather than *hamēn*, as earlier in the text.

142. Plural.

143. The references to the stars, their influences, and their eventual destruction are astrological and apocalyptic.

144. See Ezekiel 16:15-22 and also Gospel of Judas 40 on slaying children and committing fornication.

145. Here and in the following lines the text may have read "and [they will sleep with men] and [they . . .]," or the like; see Gospel of Judas 38, 40.

146. Thirteen aeons are mentioned with reference to the world below in the Holy Book of the Great Invisible Spirit and Zostrianos (the former text refers to the God of the thirteen aeons). The thirteenth aeon is referred to multiple times in the Books of Jeu and the Pistis Sophia, where it is called the place of righteousness and the dwelling place of Sophia, who descended from the thirteenth aeon and is destined to return there again. See pages 146-152 for further discussion.

147. The restoration is tentative.

148. The wandering stars are probably the five planets (Mercury, Venus, Mars, Jupiter, and Saturn) along with the Moon. According to ancient astronomical and astrological theory, such wandering stars can rule over us and influence our lives in unpleasant ways. See also Gospel of Judas 37.

JESUS SPEAKS OF THOSE WHO ARE BAPTIZED
AND JUDAS'S ACT OF HANDING HIM OVER

And Judas said to Jesus, "What will those who have been baptized in your name do?"[149]

Jesus said, "Truly I say [to you], this baptism [**56**] [. . . in] my name [—*about nine lines missing*—] to me. Truly [I] say to you, Judas, those [who] offer sacrifices to Saklas[150] [. . .] divine (?) [—*about three lines missing*—] everything that is evil.

"But you will exceed all of them. For you will sacrifice the man who bears me.[151]

> *Already your horn has been raised,*
> *and your wrath has been kindled,*
> *and your star has passed by,*
> *and your heart has [become strong].*[152] [**57**]

"Truly [I say to you], your last [. . . , . . .] become [—*about two and a half lines missing*—grie]ving [—*about two lines missing*—] the ru[ler], since he will be destroyed. [And] then will the image[153] of the great generation of Adam be exalted, for prior to heaven, earth, and the angels, that generation, which is from the aeons, exists.[154]

---

149. These are Christians baptized in the name of Christ. Whether this is meant as a criticism of ordinary Christian baptism or a recommendation of Sethian baptism, as in other Sethian texts, is unclear.

150. On offering sacrifices to Saklas, see Gospel of Judas 38-41.

151. The man who bears Jesus is the fleshly body that bears the true spiritual self of Jesus. The inner, spiritual person of Jesus will not actually die, but will be liberated. See the Second Discourse of Great Seth, the Nag Hammadi Revelation of Peter, Basilides in Irenaeus of Lyon 1.24.4, etc.

152. On the poetic lines depicting how Judas is prepared for his act of handing over the man who bears Jesus, see passages from the Psalms, for example 75:4-5, 10; 89:17, 24; 112:9; 132:17; and 148:14.

153. Coptic, from Greek, *tupos*. The text, restored to read [*tu*]*pos,* may also be restored as [*to*]*pos,* "place" (also from Greek).

154. That is, the generation of Seth is a preexistent generation that comes from God.

"Look, you have been told everything. Lift up your eyes and look at the cloud and the light within it and the stars surrounding it. And the star that leads the way is your star."

So Judas lifted up his eyes and saw the luminous cloud, and he[155] entered it.[156] Those standing on the ground[157] heard a voice coming from the cloud, saying, [*58*] "[. . . the] great gene[ration . . .] image [. . .] and [—*about five and a half lines missing*—].[158]

CONCLUSION: JUDAS HANDS JESUS OVER

[And] their high priests murmured because [. . .][159] had gone into the guest room[160] for his prayer.[161] But some of the scribes were there watching carefully in order to arrest him during

---

155. The antecedent of the pronoun "he" is ambiguous. Sasagu Arai and Gesine Schenke Robinson suggest that the pronoun may refer not to Judas but to Jesus and that it is here understood that the spiritual person of Jesus returns to the realm above and his fleshly body is left behind to be crucified.

156. This passage may be described as the transfiguration of Judas or Jesus. Judas or Jesus appears to be vindicated by being glorified in the luminous cloud, and a voice speaks from the cloud. On the luminous cloud, note may be taken of the cloud of light around the great invisible Spirit (Gospel of Judas 47) as well as other clouds in the text, sometimes for lower powers. Compare other accounts of the transfiguration of Jesus (Matthew 17:1-8, Mark 9:2-8, Luke 9:28-36; see also Book of Allogenes 61-62 in Codex Tchacos). April DeConick interprets the cloud to which Judas ascends as the thirteenth aeon, the realm of the demiurge and ruler of this world; see also the thirteenth aeon as the realm of Sophia in the Pistis Sophia.

157. Or, "below."

158. Most of the words of the divine voice from the cloud are lost in the lacuna in the manuscript, but it may be speculated that the voice may have praised Judas or Jesus or offered conclusions about the meaning of the events described. On a divine voice in the New Testament gospels, compare the accounts of the transfiguration of Jesus as well as the baptism of Jesus (Matthew 3:13-17, Mark 1:9-11, and Luke 3:21-22).

159. The lacuna may be restored as either "[he]" (that is, Jesus) or "[they]" (that is, Jesus and the disciples).

160. In Coptic, from Greek, *kataluma*. The same word is used in Mark 14:14 and Luke 22:11 for the guest room where the last supper was celebrated.

161. This clause may also be translated as direct speech: "[And] their high priests murmured, '[He] has (or, [They] have) gone into the guest room for his prayer.'"

the prayer. For they were afraid of the people, since he was regarded by all as a prophet.[162]

And they approached Judas and said to him, "What are you doing here? You are Jesus' disciple."

And he answered them as they wished.

And Judas received money and handed him over to them.[163]

The Gospel of Judas[164]

---

162. See Matthew 26:1-5, Mark 14:1-2, Luke 22:1-2, and John 11:45-53.
163. See Matthew 26:14-16, 44-56; Mark 14:10-11, 41-50; Luke 22:3-6, 45-53; and John 18:1-11. The conclusion of the Gospel of Judas is presented in subtle and understated terms, and there is no account of the crucifixion of Jesus.
164. Here the wording of the titular subscript is not "The Gospel according to (*pkata* or *kata*) Judas," as is the case in most gospel texts, but "The Gospel of (*ⁿn-*) Judas."

COMMENTARY

THE STORY OF CODEX TCHACOS AND THE GOSPEL OF JUDAS

Rodolphe Kasser

I LET OUT A CRY WHEN I SAW FOR THE FIRST TIME, ON THE EVENING OF July 24, 2001, "the object" my very embarrassed visitors had brought for me to examine. It was still a completely unknown cultural document at this date, with such a powerful text and yet written on material so frail, so sickly in appearance, so close to ultimate extinction. The papyrus codex written in Coptic, more than sixteen hundred years old, had been damaged by so many misfortunes, many of which could have been avoided. It was a stark victim of cupidity and ambition. My cry was provoked by the striking vision of the object so precious but so badly mistreated, broken up to the extreme, partially pulverized, infinitely fragile, crumbling at the least contact; the "ancient book," to which was later to be given the name "Codex Tchacos," was that evening a poor small thing pitifully packed at the bottom of a cardboard box.

How was it possible that such vandalism could occur at the dawn of the twenty-first century? How could this have happened in a milieu—one of art merchants—well-known for the gentleness of its methods and careful work? Or worse yet, in an environment even more noble and honorable, the world of scholarship?

July 24, 2001, clearly divides the history of Codex Tchacos into a "before" and "after" phase. After this date, I can tell of my own experiences. But concerning what really happened to the Codex pages before this date, I have no personal knowledge. However, the codex bears the scars of this period.

The Maecenas Foundation for Ancient Art, the current owner of the codex, which has the responsibility for safeguarding it and providing the initial publication of its content, has made a considerable effort in trying to reconstruct the "before" phase and asked Herbert Krosney to investigate and document this search independently. His zealous efforts are provided in his book, *The Lost Gospel: The Quest for the Gospel of Judas Iscariot* (National Geographic, 2006), and I have had the opportunity to take note of some of his findings.

In its present dilapidated state, Codex Tchacos probably contains parts of thirty-three folios, or sixty-six pages, paginated regularly in the numbers that survive (because of the mutilation of the folios, the numbers for pages 5, 49-53, and 61-66 have disappeared, and it is unclear whether pages 31-32 are missing or never existed). The manuscript contains at least four different tractates:

- pages 1-9, the Letter of Peter to Philip (with approximately the same text as the second tractate of Codex VIII of the Nag Hammadi library, with the same title);
- pages 10-30, "James" (with approximately the same text as the third tractate of Codex V of the Nag Hammadi library, entitled the Revelation of James and sometimes called the First Revelation of James);
- pages 33-58, the Gospel of Judas (a completely unknown text until now, though its title was mentioned by Irenaeus in his work *Against Heresies*);

- pages 59-66, a seriously damaged tractate, to the point
  that its title has been lost, but which scholars have agreed
  to designate the Book of Allogenes, from the name of the
  main character in the tractate (this tractate has no connection with the third tractate of Nag Hammadi Codex
  XI, entitled Allogenes, or Allogenes the Stranger).

DARK BIRTH FOLLOWED BY A TORMENTED CHILDHOOD:
THE EGYPTIAN AND GREEK DEALINGS

Herb Krosney reports that the codex was found during a
clandestine outing, probably around 1978, in Middle Egypt.
The linguistic patterns found in the texts of this manuscript
confirm this origin, since all of them belong to a local Middle
Egyptian variety of Sahidic (the southern supralocal Coptic
dialect). The excavator probed a tomb dug in the side of the
Jebel Qarara (east bank) of the Nile River, dominating the
village of Ambar close to Maghagha, 60 kilometers north of
Al Minya.

Antiquities dealers, whose role proved to be considerable
in this business, were contacted after this discovery. One was
an Egyptian named Hanna, who lived in Heliopolis, a suburb
northeast of Cairo. Hanna didn't know any language other
than Arabic, and had gained possession of the codex through
a colleague in Middle Egypt. Am Samiah (a pseudonym), a
friend of the discoverers of the codex, sold it to Hanna, on
whom the papyrus document made a very strong impression.

Hanna had assembled a host of precious items in his
Cairo apartment to display to a new customer, but, before the
customer returned to pay for the objects, Hanna found his
apartment emptied by nighttime robbers. The major pieces
stolen were the codex, a gold statuette of Isis, and a gold neck-
lace. In subsequent years, objects that had been stolen from

Hanna started to pop up in Europe. He decided to travel to Geneva and talk to a Greek dealer who had been regularly buying from him, to seek assistance in retrieving the stolen items. In 1982, with the Greek dealer's help, Hanna eventually succeeded in recovering the codex.

Even before the theft, Hanna had consulted several experts, probably European papyrologists, to determine how valuable the codex was, and their response prompted him to seek an extremely high selling price. We don't know exactly who gave that incautious and questionable valuation.

Immediately after its recovery, Hanna tried by all means available to him to sell his manuscript, looking for an institution endowed with sufficient financial means to meet the price he had put on his treasure. It certainly was an exalted enterprise, but one in which he was out of his depth. Eventually, Hanna succeeded in contacting Ludwig Koenen, a member of the Department of Classical Studies of the University of Michigan.

The 52 Coptic gnostic or gnosticizing treatises discovered in 1945 near Nag Hammadi in Upper Egypt, identified for the first time by Jean Doresse, had caused an exceptional interest at that time among Coptologists, historians of religion, and theologians. Between 1970 and 1980, this interest was close to its apogee. European along with American Coptologists and gnostic scholars were concluding their various contributions of research and publication in this area, and one of the leaders in this enterprise was James M. Robinson, who had helped conduct the research on Coptic gnostic manuscripts of Nag Hammadi. These scholars closely followed the European and American markets of antiquities in the hope of being able to recover (and find some sponsor or university to buy) one or another of the folios currently lost among the 13 codices of the Nag Hammadi library or more or less similar texts to those that had already been discovered and identified.

FAILURE AT GENEVA

Hanna's intriguing offer led to Koenen contacting Robinson. Koenen told him that he would go to Geneva in May 1983 to negotiate the purchase of three papyrus codices. The first, the only one that interested him, included a Greek mathematical text. The second, in Greek also, was a book of the Old Testament, and it interested one of his colleagues, David Noel Freedman, who would accompany him to Geneva. The third codex, containing only Coptic, didn't interest the others, but they supposed that it would interest Robinson. He was thus offered the opportunity to participate in these negotiations, while also contributing to the search for the funds needed to make the purchase. His answer was affirmative. Unable to go himself, Robinson sent in his place Stephen Emmel, one of his best students, along with $50,000 for the intended purchase.

That sum, along with the additional moneys available to Koenen and Freedman, was certainly substantial, but it was not even close to the amount required by Hanna for his "three" manuscripts. In fact, the third, the one in Coptic, was composed of two distinct codices, the codex of Judas' gospel and a codex containing letters of Paul; had Hanna known this, he might have used the pretext to increase his price. Even so, an abyss separated the money the scholars offered and Hanna's demand, and very quickly the negotiations broke down. He believed the texts were equal in worth to those found at Nag Hammadi. Since the media attention focused some 38 years before on the texts of Nag Hammadi had put them nearly on the same level of the famous Dead Sea Scrolls, the uproar had turned his head. The purchase was not consummated, and the three potential purchasers went back home, their hands empty.

The enterprise quickly ended in failure, because of the extraordinary price of the seller and the fact that the researchers had not been able to do anything more than glimpse discreetly the coveted text for a scant hour. Afterward, it would disappear for long years in a dark bank vault, and was in danger of vanishing completely, if some physical accident during its ill-advised journeys reduced it to dust or ashes.

Here intrudes the question of scientific morals, or deontology (any consideration of individual friendship or antipathy being put aside). A temporary lapse can be forgiven, accepting that one believes a private purchase to be a more efficient process, if it is recognized later that the chosen option had not been beneficial scientifically. The best ethical choice for the codex would have been to alert, giving them all necessary information to act, other Coptologists and gnostic scholars, even if they belonged to some "rival" side. Combined, the competing teams could have possibly located more considerable financial support, and so they would have been able to "catch the big fish." As it turns out, a few notes, in several academic publications, signaled the existence of a new gnostic witness, however in an elliptical fashion, not permitting anyone the depth of knowledge needed to approach the antiquarian possessor of the document and secure it for the researchers concerned. Some of these more precise details probably circulated "between friends," but without going beyond the confines of a very personal and confidential setting. "Cooperative deontology," if such an expression may be used, might have rescued the manuscript far earlier. Instead, scholars had to fly from the United States to Switzerland to attempt to buy a treasure that neither Swiss nor other European Coptologists had any idea existed.

At the time, the Maecenas Foundation had not yet been created, beginning only in 1994. Yet in 1982, Frieda Tchacos Nussberger, herself born in Egypt and now living in Zurich as a dealer in ancient art, had followed Hanna and his attempts to sell the codex. She received a photo of a "page 5/19" of the codex. This odd numbering for the folio came about because, already between its discovery and 1982, the energetic handling to which the manuscript had been submitted had produced a more or less horizontal deep fold, apparently affecting all of the folios, and each of them had separated into an upper fragment (about a third or a quarter of the folio) and a lower fragment (the remaining two-thirds or three-quarters of the folio). The upper fragment carried the pagination, which permitted me later to situate without hesitation the upper fragments in relation to the others, but this advantage was denied the lower fragments. In nearly all cases, a crumbling of one to two centimeters had gnawed away the folded portion, widening the gap; this prevented direct contact between the upper and lower fragments and produced a series of small fragments only millimeters in size, making it nearly impossible to identify and to fit the adjoining fragment to the one corresponding to it. The numbering in the photo of 1982 was 5/19, because whoever arranged the fragments for the photograph, mistakenly or deliberately, placed the top of page 5 with the bottom of page 19; 20 years later, as a consequence of these manipulations, the Coptologists beginning to decipher the texts of the codex had in front of them several other photos of crossed fragments, 5/13, 13/21, and so forth.

Stephen Emmel wrote a report after the 1983 inspection that reveals the respect with which he handled the papyrus text. Following the orders given by the owner, he avoided manipulating it. His report shows his obvious concern to protect to the utmost extent possible the physical structure of the codex:

> The leaves and fragments of the codex will need to be conserved between panes of glass. I would recommend conservation measures patterned after those used to restore and conserve the Nag Hammadi codices.... Despite the breakage that has already occurred, and that which will inevitably occur between now and the proper conservation of the manuscript, I estimate that it would require about a month to reassemble the fragments of the manuscript.

After having reviewed the codex for a second time 22 years later—after it had been recovered, in an imperiled state, by the Maecenas Foundation—he testified that, to his memory, in 1983 the fragmentation was relatively little advanced. This is how his earlier report described it:

> Certainly the gem of the entire collection of four manuscripts is item 2, a papyrus codex from the 4th century A.D., approximately 30 cm tall and 15 cm broad, containing gnostic texts. At the time that the codex was discovered, it was probably in good condition, with a leather binding and complete leaves with all four margins intact. But the codex has been badly handled.

It had been "badly handled" already, between the moment of its discovery and that inspection on May 15, 1983, and its condition would worsen seriously between then and 2001. He continued:

Only half of the leather binding (probably the front cover) is now preserved and the leaves have suffered some breakage. The absence of half of the binding and the fact that page numbers run only into the 50's lead me to suppose that the back half of the codex may be missing; only closer study can prove or disprove this supposition. The texts are in a non-standard form of Sahidic.... The codex contains at least three different texts: (1) "The First Apocalypse of James" known already, though in a different version, from Nag Hammadi Codex (NHC) V; (2) "The Letter of Peter to Philip" known already from NHC VIII ... ; and (3) a dialogue between Jesus and his disciples (at least "Judas" [i.e., presumably, Judas Thomas] is involved) similar in genre to "The Dialogue of the Savior" (NHC III) and "The Wisdom of Jesus Christ" (NHC III and the Berlin gnostic codex [PB 8502]).

As it turns out, "items" 1 and 2 were correctly identified (although in an incorrect order), but Emmel misunderstood who Judas was in item 3. In an article in 2005 *(Watani International)*, Robinson suggests an explanation: "The seller had forbidden his visitors to write any notes or take any photographs, but Emmel had evaded the edict surreptitiously. He excused himself to go to the bathroom, where he transcribed what his acute eye and memory had retained of the Coptic material. He afterward wrote up his notes in a confidential memorandum."

The episode makes one wonder what would have happened had Emmel, by some stratagem, been able, for several minutes at least, to investigate the codex in its owner's absence, even to photograph some characteristic passages of it. A more in-depth perusal would have likely suggested an overhaul of the report, taking into account information that he didn't possess in June 1983. Such additional information would have corrected the "mistake" on the exact title of "James" (*Iakkōbos*, not Revelation of James) and the position of the small treatise entitled the Letter of Peter to Philip, which, the pagination proves, precedes "James" in the codex.

BETWEEN 1983 AND 2001:
FURTHER AND ACCELERATED DESTRUCTION

We have little precise information about what happened to the papyri during the seventeen years that elapsed between May 15, 1983, and April 3, 2000, the date on which Frieda Tchacos Nussberger obtained possession of the codex for the first time. Through documentary evidence at the Maecenas Foundation, we know now that, on March 23, 1984, Hanna rented a safe-deposit box with Citibank in a Hicksville, New York, branch and that he kept this safe-deposit box until April 3, 2000, the date on which he sold his manuscripts to Frieda Nussberger. The inquiry conducted by Herb Krosney has shown that sometime in 1984 Hanna contacted New York manuscript dealer Hans P. Kraus, as well as Professor Roger Bagnall from Columbia University in New York, offering his manuscripts for sale. We may assume that during the subsequent years Hanna eventually understood that his asking price was too high and that he would never succeed in selling his objects at that value. The manuscripts remained all through these years enclosed in the narrow box suffering from the frequently changing but generally humid climate of this New York suburb.

On April 3, 2000, Nussberger deposited the codex for some months, for examination, in the Beinecke Library at Yale University. While there, specialists had access to it, to probe it a little in order to know its contents better. During its stay at the Beinecke Library, Bentley Layton succeeded in identifying the third treatise contained in the codex as the Gospel of Judas (Iscariot). Nevertheless, in August 2000, Yale made known that it was not going to purchase the codex.

On September 9, 2000, Nussberger sold the object to an American antiquarian named Bruce Ferrini, who is said to have frozen it, a process that lessened its integrity in a catastrophic manner. After a calamitous sojourn in the moistness of numerous American summers, this inauspicious freezing apparently produced the partial destruction of the sap holding the fibers of the papyrus together, making it significantly more fragile—and susceptible to crumbling, producing the weakest folios of papyrus that professional papyrologists had ever seen, a fragility that is a true nightmare for the restorer. Furthermore, this freezing made all the water in the fibers migrate toward the surface of the papyrus before evaporation, bringing with it quantities of pigment from inside the fibers, which darkened many pages of the papyrus and therefore made the writing extremely difficult to read.

Unable to fulfill his financial obligations to Frieda Nussberger, the antiquarian committed to return the totality of the parts of the codex in his possession, along with any transcriptions and all photos he had taken. However, later events indicated that Ferrini, after delivering the materials to Nussberger, still had several fragments of pages, at least some of which he sold elsewhere. In addition, he had many photographs of pages, providing them to the Coptologist Charles W. Hedrick.

At this point, the Swiss lawyer who had been helping Frieda Nussberger to recover her manuscripts from Ferrini suggested an acquisition of the codex by his Maecenas Foundation for Ancient Art, in Basel. Nussberger accepted his offer on the spot, and the codex was officially imported to Switzerland on February 19, 2001, in the name of the Foundation.

Consonant with its objectives, the Foundation wanted to have the codex withdrawn from the notable risks of circulating in the market; professionally restored, conserved, and published; and eventually donated to an appropriate institution in Egypt, its country of origin. Egyptian authorities have since accepted the promised donation and have designated the Coptic Museum of Cairo as the final home of the codex. These are the circumstances that led up to the meeting of July 24, 2001.

MIRACULOUS RESURRECTION: DIAGNOSIS AND FIRST MEASURES

At the beginning of July 2001, destiny (if such terminology is allowed) appeared unexpectedly, setting in motion the process that was going to transform the despaired case of Codex Tchacos—close to extinction after a long period of agony—to a case full of hope, in spite of the damage undergone, of which some had unfortunately become irreversible. The case promised to have a glorious future, as Stephen Emmel had mentioned in his report of June 1, 1983: "I strongly urge you to acquire this gnostic codex. It is of the utmost scholarly worth, comparable in every way to any one of the Nag Hammadi codices."

As a result from successive astonishing coincidences, I was called by the Maecenas Foundation. A meeting followed, in Zurich on the twenty-fourth of the month. What I had been told about the papyrus codex in question excited my curiosity, and I asked permission to see it first. I added the following proposition: If the examination of the enigmatic object proved to be positive, I could possibly advise Maecenas about the best procedures to take. If the texts written on the papyrus were sufficiently interesting, I proposed to prepare them for publication. The manuscript had to be restored meticulously and consolidated. This would not be a small business if—given the most pessimistic hypothesis—its status was considered close to total disintegration. Then every folio of the codex would be put under glass, in order to be photographed, since an essential part of the preparation of the edition would be made on the basis of excellent photographs, in order to handle the original the least amount possible. Still, it was an enticing project, stimulating, one creating enthusiasm while retaining strict standards. At the end of this process, Maecenas, in accordance with its principles, would give back to Egypt a manuscript worthy of its ancient civilization, an object provided with all the care it could need, completely restored, correctly published. This process could be considered a model of collaboration between Maecenas and the injured nation.

It would be unjust to pass over the enormous debt of recognition that the scientific community owes Maecenas for its restoration of the papyrus, the progressive photographic work, and the establishment of the conditions making possible the edition of the texts contained in the codex. If this previously luckless manuscript is resuscitated today from the black hole to which it seemed destined, with its cultural wealth completely unknown up to now, this miracle—the term is not exaggerated—Coptic scholars and theologians owe to Maecenas's exemplary perseverance in this remarkable operation.

Let us return to a narration of the events of July 24, 2001. I first saw the famous codex that evening. I expected a surprise, and it certainly was. When they showed it to me, it was huddled up at the bottom of a cardboard box—the remains of what had been a pristine papyrus codex, maybe of the first half of the fourth century. What I could see from this initial perusal of the text showed it was written in a Sahidic supralocal dialect of the Coptic language, crossed with dialectical influences evoking some local dialect of Middle Egypt. That corresponded with what I was told about the place of the discovery: the region of Al Minya. This first glance, appeasing my curiosity, was for me an electrifying experience, inviting me to guess what lay in the secret garden of the text. Sweet rapture, yes, deeply stimulating, but one followed by a brutal shock. During my long career, I have had before my eyes many Coptic or Greek documents on papyrus, sometimes very "sick," but damaged to this point, never! In many places, the papyrus was so blackened that reading had become practically impossible. The papyrus had become so weakened that it didn't tolerate the least touching; nearly all contact, as light as it was, threatened to leave it in dust. It was a case apparently without hope.

However, after the first shock, the codex's attraction became irresistible when I found one of its colophons, placed in such a way that it seemed to be on its final page, announcing a treatise considered irreparably lost: *peuaggelion nioudas*, the Gospel of Judas. This justified at least an introductory probe. And while valuing the success of the enterprise, I concluded that all didn't appear hopelessly negative. Huddled up in the box that contained it, with its fragile and broken-up folios, the codex appeared to have escaped a piecemeal scattering. Even if most of the middle part of the folios had been broken in about ten fragments, at least I could reasonably believe that they had remained concentrated in the box. By taking them out carefully, with as little disturbance as possible, then restoring, consolidating them somewhat, I would perhaps succeed, with a great deal of patience and luck as well, in pasting them together again, thus reconstituting some parts of the dismembered folios. Another reason for moderate optimism was that the upper margin of the pages seemed rather little damaged, meaning there was the possibility of continuous pagination.

That would permit me to establish successive folios, containing texts not seen in precisely this form since antiquity and belonging to an entirely new gospel. The owners of the codex accepted this preliminary verdict and offered quite generously to take care of the initial expenses.

The first necessary measure to take without delay in the restoration was setting under glass, one by one, all of the folios, including the incomplete fragments. Important parts of the binding of the codex were missing, and, apart from a few sections in the center, its folios were no longer fixed to each other. After protecting the folios this way, we could then adjust them more freely, with lower risk, photograph the pages, and finally read the text progressively, while aiming to translate the whole. This meticulous work was undertaken immediately. I need to emphasize here the expertise and dexterity that was put into this operation of incomparable difficulty and gentleness by Florence Darbre, the director of the Atelier de Restauration (Nyon), which was commissioned in this work. With her fairy-like fingers, she made largely possible what, at first glance, appeared doomed to failure. Instrumental also in our success in establishing, transcribing, translating, and commenting on the revealed text was the excellent professional work provided, at every step of the way, by photographer Christian Poite of Geneva. The quality of the pictures he obtained was an inestimable help in our struggle to identify the severely damaged letters, too often blurry because of the disastrous condition of the papyrus. Thus, the work, conducted with exactitude and tenacity, soon bore its first fruits.

Then, in 2004, I proceeded to obtain the services of an excellent collaborator in the person of Gregor Wurst, a Coptologist in his own right. Thanks to the unusually delicate work of restoration, to our investigation and assessment, it became possible to confirm what previous observers from before 2001 had been able to only glimpse, that this codex contained four successive texts. The fourth (designated the Book of Allogenes) appeared to my collaborator, Gregor Wurst, and to myself only during the year 2004. We already had received indications of its existence: An important leftover from the pagination of the codex was kept, and this preliminary observation first raised high hopes, since the number of the folios relatively well kept seemed to reach and even pass a little the figure of thirty. These hopes, however, soon would prove to be cruelly disappointed.

Indeed, as the examination of the document became more and more advanced, it became apparent that our codex, before its acquisition by Maecenas, had undergone, presumably on behalf of some of the antiquarians that had it in their possession, various imprudent, careless manipulations that often led our scientific research into error.

RESTORATION AND RECOMPOSITION

Codex Tchacos had submitted to the pressure of a hand more impatient than respectful of the fragility of the object. It is not hard to imagine a ravenous eye, greedy to see more of the text inside the hardly penetrable mass formed by the compact heap of the superimposed pieces of papyrus. All the folios of the manuscript had, alas, been broken brutally at (about) two-thirds of their height by the deep fold previously mentioned. This rupture had divided every page into two parts of unequal area. The upper fragments have the pagination and very little text. The lower fragments are evidently devoid of pagination, but their advantage is their relative wealth of coherent text. However, the violence to the whole has made it especially difficult to identify and set in the correct position the majority of the lower fragments, having lost all reliable contact with the corresponding upper portions, and with the lower fragments having been mixed up by an ill-advised hand.

The codex had been abused, reshuffled, robbed, but, I wondered, by whom? For what reason? It seemed completely unlikely and scandalous to imagine scientific researchers, in contempt of all ethical considerations, mistreating the manuscript before conducting its restoration, solely in their inconsiderate hurry to know, before hypothetical competitors, the content of these texts still unknown.

Merchants of antiquities, on the contrary, may have other priorities and interests. Certainly, they don't want to risk too much damage (or to allow damage by an auxiliary photographer) to the object they expect will fetch a good price. But "one doesn't make an omelette without breaking an egg," and they will have difficulty convincing a potential purchaser (especially if the required price is very high) if they cannot display photos of some parts of the text (colophons and other titles, decorated in a suggestive manner), exciting the buyer's curiosity. Even if it may happen that a researcher does lend his or her participation to such an operation, few would dare risk damage to the manuscript in the hope of increasing the price before a time could be planned for a wise and methodical exploration of the manuscript. The correction of this cavalier intrusion in the first half of the codex was made by the analysis of the upper and lower fragments containing the Letter of Peter to Philip and "James," for which we have, in the collection of Nag Hammadi, enough parallel texts to permit identification of the matching lower pieces. Unfortunately, the order of the Gospel of Judas's lower sections (without any parallel text available) remained much less sure. It could be determined with certainty only by the quality of the fibers of the papyrus, although more rarely we could use the negative narrative argument, when the beginning of the text of the lower fragment could absolutely not be the continuation of the text of the upper portion.

All indications gave the impression that the codex may have been shuffled about to optimize its commercial appeal—complicating the task of the investigator to the extreme. It seemed to have been reorganized quite extensively, perhaps to make it superficially more attractive, thus sharpening the curiosity of a potential customer.

In a satisfying manner, the "packet" of about thirty folios appeared to conclude with the final title—titles then normally appearing at the end—"Gospel of Judas." Symmetrically, it might have seemed appropriate to present a "pretty title" in the beginning of the packet as well, which could explain why the end of the Letter of Peter bearing the title, actually the lower part of page 9, came to be placed below the upper portion of page 1, the beginning of that letter. This intervention created, artificially, a summary of this tractate that was so compressed that it first led us into mistakes, until the moment when we noticed that the pages were out of order.

I noticed that all these seemingly arbitrary overhauls could have resulted in a promoter-illusionist still having a substantial number of the lower fragments of the Letter of Peter, as well as of others of James and the Gospel of Judas, plus some upper portions where their mutilation had made the pagination disappear, and making from it a small supplementary packet to sell. The packet would be decorated by placing the folio 29/30 on top, which was missing from the text we had. Just such a decorated page (colophon) appeared mysteriously in the catalog of a roving religious exhibition in the United States, showing a bottom fragment of page 30, containing the final title "James" (but quite shortened in relation to its "brother" of Nag Hammadi Codex V; here it is merely "James," without the mention of any "Revelation" or "Apocalypse"). The interpretations of these obvious rearrangements remain, of course, in the domain of suspicions, but if they can shock the purchasers of these missing pieces, we might be able to recover those scattered fragments to make the codex complete.

PARIS ANNOUNCEMENT

With the express authorization of the Maecenas Foundation, on July 1, 2004, in Paris at the Eighth Congress of the International Association for Coptic Studies, I announced the discovery, for the first time, of a copy (in Coptic) of "Judas' famous gospel" (mentioned by St. Irenaeus in his treatise *Against Heresies,* around the year 180, but completely hidden since then). Before the end of 2006, the *editio princeps* of all texts of Codex Tchacos may be published. The edition should contain top-quality, full-size color photographs of all the pages of this codex. These are to be supplemented by the reproduction, also in color, of those fragments of papyrus (unfortunately very numerous) that, during the reasonable time granted by Maecenas to avoid delaying too long the publication of the already relatively legible written surfaces, have not yet been placed. These pieces will not be fully identified and placed in their place of origin without considerable future efforts. Thus, identified or not, no remnant of this famous codex would be excluded from its *editio princeps.* These fragments, irreplaceable because of their authenticity, will remain in waiting in this photographic conservatory, because, little by little, they will be identified by zealous and shrewd readers during the future decades. Generations to come will also possess more efficient methods and techniques than ours today.

One of the processes we have used to identify the remnants is the meticulous cutting, requiring infinite patience, of the color photographs of these precious fragments. The cutting has been done by volunteering hands belonging to Mireille Mathys, Serenella Meister, and Bettina Roberty. Having participated in this manner to the resurrection of Codex Tchacos, they also deserve the full recognition of the researchers that, from now on, will enjoy access to the text. While we are thanking all persons of goodwill who have contributed generously to our work but aren't mentioned on the title page, it would be unfair to omit the name of Michel Kasser, who has helped to solve various problems of decipherment of difficult photographic documents and who has prepared the English version of preliminary comments originally edited in French.

After my announcement, I waited for reactions of the audience, but only one, James Robinson, asked to speak. One of the most formidable organizers of working teams in gnostic studies, he publicly cautioned me to inquire about the existence of photographs of the codex that had been circulating in the United States for the last twenty years and which might contain part of the text that Maecenas was missing. This public warning had little effect in Paris, and most American and Canadian scholars I met there declared that they were not aware of such a situation.

But some months later, in December 2004, another American Coptologist, Charles Hedrick, greatly committed in research and publications to gnostic scholarship, sent me his transcription and translation of the lower and main fragments of pages 40 and 54-62 of the codex. The same paragraphs were simultaneously published on the Internet. These transcriptions had been made from photographs he had received.

He didn't name his source, or the date when he had obtained these photographs, but the published documents bore in the upper right-hand corner of the pages the following handwritten identification: "Transcription — translation — Gospel of Judas — 9 Sept 2001 — . . . — photographs Bruce Ferrini." This proves that the American antiquarian had failed in his agreement of February 2001 with Frieda Tchacos Nussberger by not having delivered *all photographs* and documentation he had of the codex. Moreover, it also suggests that, contrary to scholarly prudence, Ferrini or someone with access to the codex had forced open the codex in various places to photograph ten "good pages," thus accelerating its fragmentation. How many hours have been wasted to repair (or, more often, to attempt to repair) damage that should never have occurred! Herb Krosney's book has a more detailed account of the sufferings of the codex.

The text of the Gospel of Judas presented in this edition, although incomplete, offers to anyone interested in this apocryphal work a largely coherent message, whatever the textual losses due to the bad treatment of Codex Tchacos. Judas has endured the dogged ignorance of some of our contemporaries. It has suffered a material loss by erosion estimated at 10 to 15 percent. However, its message has survived largely intact. We have today a clear enough understanding of the "gospel" or "statement" conveyed a long time ago by this voice lost to world literature, thanks to a conjunction of luck and acts of goodwill and in spite of evident ethical failures. Such a spirit is not always obvious in these materialistic times, through which our soul tries to pave a track of hope. Yet a priceless document that was nearly lost to us has at last been saved.

It gives us reasons to laugh, as does the august Jesus put onstage in this literary creation of a very unusual kind. We smile at the educational dialogues of the "Master" (Rabbi) with his disciples of limited spiritual intelligence, and even with the most gifted among them, the human hero of this "Gospel," Judas the misunderstood—whatever his weaknesses. We also have reasons to smile rather than to moan at the message previously lost to us, miraculously resuscitated, emerging today from its long silence.

THE ALTERNATIVE VISION
OF THE GOSPEL OF JUDAS

Bart D. Ehrman

IT IS NOT EVERY DAY THAT A BIBLICAL DISCOVERY ROCKS THE WORLD OF
scholars and lay people alike, making front page news throughout Europe and America. The last time it happened was more
than a generation ago. The Dead Sea Scrolls were discovered
in 1947 and yet they continue to be discussed in the news and
to play a role in our collective popular imagination today. So
too with the gnostic writings discovered near Nag Hammadi,
Egypt, in December 1945 by a group of illiterate farmhands
digging for fertilizer. Hidden in a jar buried by a boulder next
to a cliff face, these writings include previously unknown
gospels, books that purportedly record the teachings of Jesus
himself in words quite different from those found in the New
Testament. Some of these gospels are anonymous, including
one called the Gospel of Truth; others were allegedly written
by Jesus' closest followers, including the Gospel of Philip and,
most remarkably, the Gospel of Thomas, which consists of
114 sayings of Jesus, many of them previously unknown.

The Gospel of Thomas may well be the most remarkable
discovery of Christian antiquity in modern times. But now
another gospel has appeared, one that rivals Thomas for its
inherent intrigue, because this one is also connected with one

of Jesus' closest intimates and contains teachings far removed from those that eventually came to be canonized in the writings of the New Testament. In this instance, however, we are not talking about a disciple known for his undying devotion to Jesus. Just the contrary, it is the one disciple reputed to be his mortal enemy and ultimate betrayer, Judas Iscariot.

For centuries there were rumors that such a gospel existed, but we did not know what it contained until its recent discovery. This discovery will undoubtedly rank among the greatest finds from Christian antiquity in modern times and the most important archaeological discoveries of the past 60 years.

Other discoveries made since the Nag Hammadi findings of 1945 have been of interest almost exclusively to scholars wanting to know more about the beginning years of Christianity. The Gospel of Judas, on the other hand, will be fascinating to the non-scholar as well, because this is a gospel about a figure who is widely known, much maligned, and broadly speculated about.

What has already made the newly published gospel famous—or, perhaps, infamous—is that its portrayal of Judas is quite different from anything we previously knew. For here he is not the evil, corrupt, devil-inspired follower of Jesus who betrayed his master by handing him over to his enemies. He is Jesus' closest friend, the one who understood Jesus better than anyone else, who turned Jesus over to the authorities because Jesus *wanted* him to do so. In handing him over he did Jesus the greatest service imaginable. According to this gospel Jesus wanted to escape this material world that stands opposed to God and return to his heavenly home. Judas made it all possible.

This gospel has a completely different understanding of God, the world, Jesus, salvation, human existence—not to mention of Judas himself—than what came to be embodied in the orthodox Christian cannon and creeds. It opens up new vistas for understanding Jesus and the religious movement he founded. And so, in this essay, I will explore three related topics: What is the distinctive portrayal of Judas in this gospel? How does its overall religious perspective differ from the "orthodox" views that came to be embraced by the majority of Christians? And why was it, and other books like it, eventually excluded from the canon of Christian Scripture?

JUDAS IN THE GOSPELS OF THE NEW TESTAMENT

There are several people named Judas in the New Testament, just as there are several Marys, several Herods, and several people named James. Since so many people had the same name, and since lower-class people never had last names, these various persons had to be distinguished from one another in some way. Usually this was done by indicating where they came from or to whom they were related. And so, for example, the different Marys are called Mary the mother of Jesus, Mary of Bethany, Mary Magdalene, etc. Among those named Judas—or Jude, as the name is sometimes translated—one was an actual brother of Jesus (Matthew 13:55); another was a disciple, Judas the son of James (Luke 6:16); and yet a third was another disciple, Judas Iscariot. Scholars have long debated what "Iscariot" is supposed to mean, and no one knows for sure. It may refer to Judas' home town, a village in Judea (in the southern part of modern Israel) called Kerioth ("Ish-Kerioth," or Iscariot, would mean "man from Kerioth"). In any event, when I refer to Judas here in this discussion, it will always be to this one, Judas Iscariot, best known for his ignominious act of betraying Jesus to the authorities before his crucifixion.

As I have already suggested, Judas' betrayal is not portrayed as an ignominious act in the Gospel of Judas. But, in the New Testament gospels, this is his distinguishing mark. Among the twelve disciples, he is the bad apple, the nefarious betrayer. Judas is mentioned some 20 times in these books, and in every instance the gospel writers have something hostile to say about him, usually simply pointing out that he was Jesus' betrayer. They all assume this was a very bad thing.

Readers over the years have wondered about that. If Jesus had to die on the cross for the salvation of the world, then wasn't Judas doing a *good* thing in handing him over? Without the betrayal there would be no arrest, without the arrest there would be no trial, without the trial there would be no crucifixion, without the crucifixion there would be no resurrection—and in short, we *still* wouldn't be saved from our sins. So why were Judas' actions such a bad thing?

The New Testament writers never answer that speculative question. They simply state that Judas betrayed the cause and his master and that, even though something good came out of it, his act was a damnable offense: "It would have been better for that man never to have been born!" (Mark 14:21).

These canonical accounts provide different explanations for why Judas did what he did. The first of our gospels was probably Mark, and in that account we are given no explanation of the deed at all: Judas goes to the Jewish leaders volunteering to betray Jesus, and they agree to give him some money in exchange (Mark 14:10-11). It may be that Judas wanted the money, but Mark doesn't say that was his motivation. The Gospel of Matthew, written some years after Mark, is more explicit: In this account Judas approaches the Jewish leaders to see how much he can make off of his act of betrayal;

they settle the amount at thirty pieces of silver, and he keeps his end of the bargain. Here Judas' motive is greed (Matthew 26:14-16). The Gospel of Luke, written at about the same time as Matthew, throws in an additional factor: Satan—the ultimate enemy of God—entered into Judas and drove him to do the dirty deed (Luke 22:3). In this account, Judas could say, "The devil made me do it." The last gospel to be written is John, and in it we learn that Jesus knew all along that "one of you (disciples) is a devil" (John 6:70). Moreover, we're told that Judas had been entrusted with the group's treasure chest (John 12:4-6) and commonly used to dip into it for his own purposes. For this gospel, then, Judas is driven both by his own evil, demonic nature and by greed.

What is it, exactly, that Judas betrayed to the authorities? On this the New Testament gospels appear to agree. Jesus and his disciples had come from the northern part of the land to the capital city, Jerusalem, in order to celebrate the annual Passover feast. This was an important event in Jerusalem at the time, since during the festival the population of the city would swell many times over as pilgrims from around the world came together to worship God in commemoration of the act of salvation he had performed, many centuries before, when Moses led the children of Israel out of their slavery in Egypt. There were enormous crowds, and there was always the fear of religious enthusiasm growing to a fevered pitch and leading to riots. The authorities were particularly afraid that Jesus might be a troublemaker, and they wanted to have him arrested away from the crowds, quietly, so that they could dispose of him without creating a major disturbance. Judas was the one who told them how they could do it. He led them to Jesus in the dead of night when he was alone, with his disciples, praying. The authorities made the secret arrest, put Jesus on trial before a kangaroo court, and had him crucified before any real resistance could be organized.

What happened next, to Judas, is recounted by only two of our gospel writers. Most famously, according to the Gospel of Matthew, Judas was filled with remorse, returned the thirty pieces of silver to the Jewish authorities, and went out to hang himself. The authorities realized they could not use the returned money for the temple treasure, since it had been used to betray innocent blood. And so they purchased a field with it, to use for the burial of strangers. The field was called a potter's field, possibly because it contained red clay popular among the potters in town. It came then to be known as "the Field of Blood" because it had been purchased with "blood money."

Mark and John don't say anything about Judas' demise, nor does the Gospel of Luke. But in the book of Acts—written by the author of Luke, as a kind of sequel to his gospel—we also learn about Judas' death, and it again is tied to a field in Jerusalem. In this case, however, Judas himself is said to have purchased the field and to have died on it. Here he does not hang himself. Instead, he bursts forth in the midst (i.e., his stomach rips open) and he spills his intestines on the ground, creating a bloody mess. It is for *that* reason called the "Field of Blood" (Acts 1:15-19). This does not appear to be a suicide, as in Matthew, but an act of God, who brings Judas to a gory end in just retribution for his evil deed.

JUDAS IN THE GOSPEL OF JUDAS

All of these accounts stand in stark contrast with what we find in the Gospel of Judas. Here Judas' deed is not evil. Instead, he does the will of God, as explained to him in secret revelations by Jesus himself. By making it possible for Jesus to die, Judas allows the divine spark within Jesus to escape the material trappings of his body to return to his heavenly home. Judas is the hero of the account, not the villain.

Already in the opening words of this gospel it becomes clear that the portrayal of Judas will not be at all like that found in the New Testament and that the account that follows will contain a gnostic perspective on his deed. For the text begins by indicating that it is "the secret word of the declaration by which Jesus spoke in conversation with Judas Iscariot." Off the bat, then, we're told that this is a "secret" account—it is not for everyone, but only for those who are in the know, that is, for "gnostics." The account conveys a revelation given by Jesus, the divine emissary who alone can reveal the truth necessary for salvation. And to whom does he reveal it? Not to the crowds who flock to hear him teach, not even to the twelve disciples he has called around him. He reveals the secret to Judas Iscariot alone, his most intimate companion, and the only one in this gospel who understands the real truth of Jesus.

The next time Judas is mentioned in the text is on manuscript page 35, where Jesus challenges the twelve disciples to show whether or not they are "perfect" (that is, capable of salvation) and stand before him. The disciples all claim that they have the strength to do so, but in fact it is only Judas who is able to stand, and even he has to turn his face away. This appears to mean that Judas has the spark of the divine within him, so that he is in some sense on par with Jesus (he can stand before him), but he has not yet come to understand the secret truth that Jesus is about to reveal, and so he averts his eyes. But Judas does know Jesus' true identity—something the others are completely blind to. For Judas proclaims that Jesus is not a mere mortal from this world. He comes from the divine world above: "You have come from the immortal aeon of Barbelo," he says. As Marvin Meyer explains in his essay, according to Sethian gnostics, Barbelo is one of the primary divine beings in the perfect realm of the true God. That is where Jesus has come from—not from this world created by a secondary, inferior, ignorant deity.

Because Judas has correctly perceived Jesus' character, Jesus takes him aside, away from the ignorant others, to teach him "the mysteries of the kingdom." Judas alone will receive the secret knowledge necessary for salvation. And Jesus informs him that he will attain to this salvation, even though he will grieve in the process. He will grieve because he will be rejected by "the twelve," who will elect someone to take his place. This is a reference to what happens in the New Testament book of Acts, when after Judas' death, the eleven disciples replace him with Matthias, so that they can remain twelve in number (Acts 1:16-26). For the Gospel of Judas, this is a good thing— not for the twelve but for Judas. He is the one who can attain salvation, while the other apostles continue to be concerned about "their God"—that is, the creator-God of the Old Testament, whom both Jesus and Judas can transcend.

This theme is replayed later in the text, when Judas recounts to Jesus a "great vision" that he has seen that has troubled him. In this vision he saw the twelve disciples (evidently the eleven others and the one who eventually would replace him) stoning him to death. But then he saw a great house filled with magnificent people. Judas wants to enter that house— because, in fact, the house represents the divine realm where the immortal spirits dwell in eternal harmony. Jesus informs him that no one who is born of mortals can enter that house: "It is reserved for the holy." But as is suggested later in the text, this means that everyone—like Judas—who has a spark of the divine within will be allowed entrance, once they have escaped their mortal flesh (53).

Judas' impending death, in other words, will not be a great disaster, even though he might find it grievous at the time. For upon his death he will become the "thirteenth," that is, he will be outside the number of the twelve disciples and will transcend their number. He alone will be able to enter into the divine realm symbolized by the great house of his vision. And so he will "be cursed by the other generations," by the race of mortals who are not destined for ultimate salvation. At the same time, he "will come to rule over them," for he will be far superior to all in this material world, once he has attained to his salvation, based on the secret knowledge that Jesus is about to reveal (46).

A good portion of the surviving gospel contains the secret revelation that Jesus delivers to Judas alone. It is a revelation about "a great and boundless aeon"—the eternal realm of the truly divine beings beyond this world and far above the inferior deities who created this material existence and humans. The revelation will strike many modern readers as inordinately complex and difficult to understand. But its basic thrust is clear. Numerous superior divine beings came into existence long before the gods of this world appeared. The gods of this world include El (the word for "God" in the Old Testament); his helper Nebro, also called Yaldabaoth, who is defiled with blood and whose name means "rebel"; and another god named Saklas, a word that means "fool." Thus the deities in charge of this world are the Old Testament God, a bloody rebel, and a fool. This is not a ringing endorsement of the world or its creator(s).

Saklas, the fool, is said to be the one who creates humans "after the [his own?] image" (52). Which leads Judas to question: Is it possible for humans to transcend life in this world? As we will see later, the answer is a qualified Yes. Some humans have an element of the divine within. They will survive to transcend this world, to enter into the divine realm far above the blood-thirsty foolish creator gods.

Judas himself is the first to do so. We're told near the end of the text that Judas has his wish fulfilled: He enters into "the luminous cloud" which represents, in this text, the world of the true God and his aeons. Like everyone else, Judas has a guiding "star." His star is superior to all the others. His star "leads the way."

And the way it leads is through his proper understanding of all that Jesus has taught him. Salvation does not come by worshiping the God of this world or accepting his creation. It comes by denying this world and rejecting the body that binds us to it. That is the ultimate reason why the deed that Judas performs for Jesus is a righteous act, one that earns him the right to excel all the others. By handing Jesus over to the authorities, Judas makes it possible for Jesus to escape his own mortal flesh to return to his eternal home. And so we have the key line of the entire text, where Jesus informs Judas: "You will exceed all of them. For you will sacrifice the man who bears me" (56). Jesus needs to escape this material world once and for all by being removed from his mortal body. And Judas is praised for making it happen.

The betrayal scene itself is told in muted terms, and it differs in a number of ways from the accounts found in the New Testament. In this account Jesus is not outside, praying in the Garden of Gethsemane, for example. He is indoors, in a "guest room." As in the New Testament gospels, the Jewish leaders, here called "the scribes," want to arrest Jesus privately, "for they were afraid of the people, since he was regarded by all as a prophet." But when they see Judas, they are surprised: "What are you doing here? You are Jesus' disciple" (58). These leaders, too, do not understand the truth, that to be Jesus' disciple means to hand him over to the authorities so that he can be executed. Judas gives them the response they want to hear, they give him some money for the deed, and he hands Jesus over. And that's where the gospel ends, with what for this author was the climax of the account: not Jesus' death and resurrection, but the faithful act of his one most intimate companion and faithful follower, the one who handed him over to his death that he might return to his heavenly home.

THE UNUSUAL THEOLOGICAL VIEWS OF THE GOSPEL OF JUDAS

We have already noticed some of the key theological themes of this gospel: The creator of this world is not the one true God; this world is an evil place to be escaped; Christ is not the son of the creator; salvation comes not through the death and resurrection of Jesus but through the revelation of secret knowledge that he provides. These themes stand diametrically opposed to the theological views that eventually "won out" in the early Christian debates concerning proper belief—that is to say, in the theological wars of the second and third Christian centuries, when different Christian groups maintained different systems of belief and doctrine, all of them insisting that their views were not only right, but were the views of Jesus and his closest followers.

We have long known about these debates, and the Gospel of Judas allows us to see one side of them even more clearly— one of the sides, in fact, that ended up losing. Every side laid claim to sacred books supporting their points of view; all insisted that these views came straight from Jesus, and through him from God. But only one side won. This was the side that decided which books should be considered scripture and that wrote the Christian creeds that have come down to us today.

Embodied in these creeds are theological statements that trumpet the success of the "orthodox" party. Consider the opening of one of the most famous of these creeds: We believe in one God, the Father, the almighty, maker of heaven and earth, of all things visible and invisible. This affirmation stands in stark contrast with the views set forth in the Gospel of Judas, where there is not just one God but many Gods, and where the creator of this world is not the true God, but an inferior deity, who is not the Father of all and is certainly not almighty.

We are now in a position to look more closely at some of the key teachings of this gospel, its views about God, the world, Christ, salvation, and the other apostles who stand behind the creed that came to be accepted as authoritative yet who never do understand the truth.

THE VIEW OF GOD IN THE GOSPEL

At the outset of the gospel it is clear that the God of Jesus is not the creator God of the Jews. In one of the opening scenes, Jesus finds the disciples gathered together "practicing their piety." Literally the Coptic says that the disciples were "training their piety." They were, in fact, having a eucharistic meal, in which they were thanking God (Greek: *eukharistō*) for their food. One would expect Jesus to respect this religious act. But instead he begins to laugh. The disciples don't see why it is funny: "Why are you laughing at [our] prayer of thanksgiving? . . . This is what is right." Jesus replies that they don't know what they are really doing: By giving thanks for their food, they are praising *their* God—that is, not the God of Jesus. Now the disciples are befuddled: "Master, you [. . .] are the son of our God." No, as it turns out, he is not. Jesus responds that no one of their "generation" will know who he really is.

The disciples do not take kindly to this rebuke and start "getting angry and . . . blaspheming against him in their hearts" (34). Jesus proceeds to upbraid them, and speaks again about "your God who is within you." Several key themes are at play here, which will repeat themselves throughout the narrative. The disciples of Jesus do not know who he really is; they worship the God who is not Jesus' father; they don't understand the truth about God. Judas, as we have seen, is the only one who truly understands. As Judas declares, Jesus has come from "the immortal aeon of Barbelo," that is, from the realm of the true immortal divine beings, not from the lower realm of the creator-God of the Jews.

This understanding of the creator-God as an inferior deity is most clearly stated in the myth that Jesus expounds privately to Judas later in the text. According to proto-orthodox writers like Irenaeus, there is only one God and he is the one who made all that exists, in heaven and earth. Not for this text, though. The complexities of the myth that Jesus reveals to Judas may seem befuddling, but its gist is clear. Even before the creator-God came into being, there were enormous numbers of other divine beings: 72 aeons, each with a "luminary" and each with five firmaments of the heavens (for a total of 360 firmaments), along with countless myriads of angels worshiping each one. Moreover, this world belongs to the realm of "corruption" (50). It is not the good creation of the one true God. Only after all the other divine entities come into existence does the God of the Old Testament, named El, come into being, and then his helpers, the blood-stained rebel Yaldabaoth and the fool Saklas. It was these later two who created the world and then humans.

When the disciples worship "their" God, it is the rebel and fool they worship, the makers of this bloody, senseless, material existence. They do not worship the true God, the one who is above all else, who is all-knowing, all-powerful, entirely spirit, completely removed from this transient world of pain and suffering. It is no wonder that Irenaeus found this text so offensive. It claimed to represent the views of Jesus, yet its views are a complete mockery of Irenaeus's most cherished beliefs.

THE VIEW OF JESUS

Throughout this text Jesus speaks of the twelve disciples and "their" God. It is clear that Jesus does not belong to the God of this world—one of his goals, in fact, is to reveal the inferiority and moral turpitude of this God, before returning to the divine realm, the perfect world of the Spirit, after leaving his mortal body. For this text, then, Jesus is not a normal human being. The first thing said about him is that he "appeared on earth." This already suggests that he came from another realm. And since he spends much of the gospel revealing the "secret mysteries" about the immortal world of true divinity, the natural assumption is that this other realm is where he originated.

His unique character is hinted at in the next comment about him: "often he does not appear to his disciples (as himself), but you find him among them [as a child]" (33). Scholars who are familiar with a range of early Christian literature will have no trouble understanding this allusion. There are a number of Christian writings outside the New Testament that portray Jesus as a "docetic" being—that is, as one who looked human only because it was an appearance (docetic comes from the Greek word *dokeō*, which means to "seem" or to "appear"). As a divine being, Jesus could take on whatever shape or form he wanted. And so in some early Christian writings Jesus could appear as an old man or a child—simultaneously, to different people! (This can be found, for example, in a non-canonical book called the Acts of John.) So too here: Jesus did not have a real fleshly body, but could assume different appearances at will.

But why would he appear to the disciples as a child? Wouldn't this appearance undercut rather than assert his authority over them? (He's just a child, what does *he* know?) This is a point that will no doubt be debated by scholars of the text for a long time. It does appear that being a child here is not meant at all in a negative way but positively: Children are unspoiled by the harsh realities of this material world and uncorrupted by its false wisdom. Moreover, doesn't the Bible itself indicate that "out of the mouth of babes you have established strength" (Psalm 8:2)? The child represents purity and innocence before the world. And Christ alone embodied absolute purity—and wisdom and knowledge that transcend the mere mortal.

This knowledge is, of course, the main theme of the Gospel of Judas. It is the knowledge of the secret mysteries that Jesus alone has and that Judas alone is worthy to hear. Jesus has this knowledge because he comes from the aeon of Barbelo. And he is shown to return to visit that realm at will. The day after his first conversation with the disciples they want to know where he had gone in the meantime, and he tells them: "I went to another great and holy generation." When they ask him about that "generation," he laughs again, this time not at their ignorant worship of the creator but at their lack of knowledge about the realm of the truly divine, because no mere mortal can go there: It is a realm beyond this world, the realm of all perfection and truth, the ultimate destination of those who contain an element of the divine that can escape the trappings of this material world. Jesus alone knows about this realm, because that is whence he came and whither he will return.

As we have seen, Judas is the most intimate follower of Jesus in this text not only because he is the only one worthy to receive the secret mysteries of that realm, but also because he makes it possible for Jesus to return there permanently. He does this by turning him over to the authorities for execution. For Jesus too—even though he only appears to have a real flesh and blood body—is for the time being here on earth in human form. He needs to escape this mortal coil to return to his heavenly home.

What then is the significance of Jesus' death in this gospel? Irenaeus and other proto-orthodox writers based their views on writings that eventually became the New Testament, such as the Gospel of Mark and the letters of the apostle Paul, where Jesus' death is said to be an atoning sacrifice for sins (see Mark 10:45 and Romans 3:21-28). In this proto-orthodox view Jesus' death was all-important for salvation: It paid the price of sin so that others—those who committed sins against God—could be restored to a right relationship with the God who created this world and all that is in it. Not so for the Gospel of Judas. In this gospel there is no need to be reconciled with the creator of this world, who is a bloodthirsty rebel. The need is to escape this world and its creator. That happens once one relinquishes the body that belongs to the creator. Jesus' death is his own escape. And when we die, we too can escape.

It will strike many readers as odd that the Gospel of Judas ends where it does, with the so-called betrayal. But it makes perfect sense given the views otherwise advanced in the book. The death of Jesus is a foregone conclusion: All that is needed is the means by which it will occur, and Judas does his part in making sure it will happen. That's why he "exceeds" all the others.

And there will be no resurrection. This is perhaps the key point of all. Jesus will not be raised from the dead in this book. Why would he be? The entire point of salvation is to escape this material world. A resurrection of a dead corpse brings the person back into the world of the creator. But if the point is to allow the soul to leave this world behind and to enter into "that great and holy generation"—that is, the divine realm that transcends this world—then a resurrection of the body is the very last thing that Jesus, or any of his true followers, would want. Jesus is to die and escape; he is not to die and rise again.

VIEW OF SALVATION

And that, of course, is the goal of Jesus' true followers as well. This world and all its trappings are to be transcended. That can happen when the soul learns the truth of its origin and destination, and then escapes from the material prison of the body.

This teaching becomes clear in a key conversation between Judas and Jesus, in which "this" generation—that is, the race of people here on earth—is contrasted with "that" generation—the realm of the divine beings. Some people belong to this generation, some to that one. It is those with the divine element within who belong to that one; only they can be saved when they die. When the others—those of "this" generation—die, that will be the end of their story. As Jesus says: "The souls of every human generation will die. When *these* people [i.e., those who belong to the realm above], however, have completed the time of the kingdom and the spirit leaves them, their bodies will die, but their souls will be alive, and they will be taken up" (43, emphasis added).

In this understanding of things, humans consist of a body, a spirit, and a soul. The body is the material part that clothes the inner soul, which is the real essence of the person. The spirit is the force that animates the body, giving it life. When the spirit leaves the body, the body dies and ceases to exist. For those who belong only to this human realm, the soul then dies as well. As Jesus later says, "It is impossible to sow seed on [rock] and harvest its fruit" (43-44). In other words, without a spark of the divine within, there will be no ongoing life. But for those who belong to the realm above, the soul lives on after death, and is taken up to its heavenly home.

This idea is further explained after Jesus describes the myth of beginnings to Judas, who wants to know "Does the human spirit die?" (53). Jesus explains that there are two kinds of human, those whose bodies have been given a spirit on a temporary basis by the archangel Michael, "so that they might offer service," and those who have eternal spirits granted them by the archangel Gabriel, who belong therefore to "the great generation with no ruler over it" (53). These latter are those who have a spark of the divine within them who, after their death, will return to the realm whence they came. Judas himself, of course, is among them. The other disciples, on the other hand, appear to be of the first kind, who out of ignorance "offer service," but who, upon their deaths, simply cease to exist.

VIEW OF JESUS' FOLLOWERS

One of the most striking features of the Gospel of Judas is this persistent refrain that the twelve disciples of Jesus never understand the truth, stand outside the realm of the saved, and persecute Judas, not realizing that it is he alone who both knows and understands Jesus and the secrets he has revealed. It is because they don't know any better, as we have seen, that they stone Judas in a vision. Judas is outside their number, and so Jesus calls him "the thirteenth." Here, thirteen is the lucky number.

The twelve disciples are portrayed as those who ignorantly worship the creator-God, for example, in the Eucharist scene that opens the account. This portrayal is even more graphic in a later scene that is so regrettably fragmentary, in which the disciples describe to Jesus a vision they themselves have had of the sacrifices taking place in the temple in Jerusalem.

Many readers will be familiar with the New Testament story of the disciples and Jesus arriving at the temple just a week before Jesus' execution. Jesus creates a disturbance in the temple, overthrowing the tables of the money changers and driving out those selling sacrificial animals (Mark 11:15-17). The disciples, on the other hand, are shown as being unduly impressed with what they have seen, as rural Galileans making a trip to the big city for the first time, and overawed by the grandeur and magnitude of the temple. As they exclaim in Mark 13:1, "Master, what large stones and what large buildings!"

The Gospel of Judas presents an alternate version of this scene. Here the disciples comment to Jesus not about the temple building but about the sacrifices taking place within it. They see an altar, priests, a crowd, and sacrifices being made, and they are disturbed, wanting to know what it is all about. As it turns out, it is all about them. Jesus tells them that the priests at the altar, performing the sacrifices, "invoke my name." In other words, those responsible for this worship of the Jewish God believe that they are serving Jesus himself. We then learn that what the disciples have seen is a symbolic vision—not about the actual Jewish sacrifices in the temple, but about their own practices of worship, because Jesus tells them: "It is you who are presenting the offerings on the altar you have seen. That one is the God you serve, and you are the twelve men you have seen. And the cattle that are brought in are the sacrifices you have seen— that is, the many people you lead astray. . ." (39). In other words, the disciples who continue to practice their religion as if the ultimate object of worship is the creator-God of the Jews, who invoke Jesus' name in support of their worship, have gotten it all wrong. Rather than serving the true God they are blaspheming him. And in doing so, they lead their followers astray.

This is a damning portrayal not only of Jesus' disciples, but also of the proto-orthodox Christians living at the time the Gospel of Judas was produced. The proto-orthodox did not, of course, continue to worship in the Jewish temple. It had been destroyed by this time and the vast majority of the proto-orthodox were Gentiles, not Jews. But they insisted that the God they worshiped was the Jewish God who gave the Jewish law and sent the Jewish Messiah to the Jewish people in fulfillment of the Jewish Scriptures. They understood themselves to be the "true Jews," the true people of the one true God.

Jesus in this gospel indicates that they are completely misled. They do indeed worship the Jewish God. But this God is a reckless fool. He did create this world, but the world is not good. It is a cesspool of misery and suffering. The true God has never had anything to do with this world. This world must be escaped, not embraced. The proto-orthodox Christians are promoting a false religion. Only the religion taught secretly by Jesus to his most intimate follower, Judas, is ultimately true. All the rest is a sham at best, a noxious error promoted by the leaders of the proto-orthodox churches.

THE GOSPEL OF JUDAS AND THE CANON OF SCRIPTURE

In light of its harsh attacks on the proto-orthodox church leaders—forebears of Irenaeus and other like-minded theologians who developed the "orthodox" way of understanding God, the world, Christ, and salvation—it is no wonder that this Gospel of Judas never had much of a chance of getting into the New Testament. In this final section, I will discuss briefly how we got our New Testament, with its four Gospels of Matthew, Mark, Luke, and John, and how it is that, whereas some few Christian writings made it into the canon, most others (like the Gospel of Judas) came to be excluded.

The New Testament consists of 27 books that the victorious orthodox party accepted as sacred texts conveying God's word to his people. When Christianity started out—with the historical Jesus himself—it already had a set of sacred written authorities. Jesus was a Jew living in Palestine, and like all Palestinian Jews, he accepted the authority of the Jewish Scriptures, especially the first five books of what Christians have called the Old Testament (Genesis, Exodus, Leviticus, Numbers, and Deuteronomy), sometimes known as the Law of Moses. Jesus in fact presented himself as an authoritative interpreter of these Scriptures and was known to his followers as a great rabbi ("teacher").

After Jesus' death, his followers continued to revere his teachings, and began to ascribe to them an authority equal to that of Moses himself. Not just Jesus' teachings, but the teachings of his closest followers were seen as authoritative, especially as these came to be written down in books. But as years and decades passed, more and more writings appeared, claiming to be written by apostles. There were the letters of Paul, for example. But we have more letters by Paul than the thirteen that go under his name in the New Testament; and many scholars have even concluded that some of those in the New Testament were not actually written by Paul. Similarly, we have the Revelation of John in the New Testament, but other apocalypses were left out of it—for example an Apocalypse of Peter and an Apocalypse of Paul.

And then of course there were lots of gospels. The four found in the New Testament may have been anonymous writings; the earliest copies do not explicitly name their authors. Only in the second century did they come to be called by the names of Jesus' disciples (Matthew and John) and of two companions of the apostles (Mark, the companion of Peter, and Luke, the companion of Paul). Other gospels appeared that claimed to be written by apostles. Even today, in addition to our newly discovered Gospel of Judas, we have gospels purportedly written by Philip and by Peter, two different gospels by Jesus' brother, Judas Thomas, one by Mary Magdalene, and so on. All of these gospels (and epistles, apocalypses, etc.) were connected with apostles; they all claimed to represent the true teachings of Jesus; they all were seen, by one Christian group or another, as Sacred Scripture. And as time went on, more and more started to appear. Given the enormous debates that were being waged over the proper interpretation of the religion, how were people to know what to believe and which books to accept?

To make a long story very short: One of the competing groups in Christianity succeeded in overwhelming all the others. This group gained more converts than its opponents and succeeded in relegating all its competitors to the margins. This group decided on what the church's organizational structure would be like. It decided which creeds Christians would recite. And it decided which books would be accepted as Scripture. This was the group to which Irenaeus belonged, as did other figures well-known to scholars of second- and third-century Christianity, such as Justin Martyr and Tertullian. It was this group that became "orthodox," and once it had sealed its victory over all of its opponents, it rewrote the history of the engagement—claiming that it had always been the majority opinion of Christianity, that its views had always been the views of the apostolic churches and of the apostles, and that its creeds were rooted directly in the teachings of Jesus. The books that it accepted as Scripture proved the point, because Matthew, Mark, Luke, and John all tell the story as the proto-orthodox had grown accustomed to hearing it.

What happened to the other books, the ones that told a different version of the story and so had been left outside of the proto-orthodox canon? Some of them were destroyed, but most of them were simply lost or worn out of existence. They were rarely if ever copied after a time, since their views had been deemed "heretical." Only in small, marginal groups within Christianity—a gnostic group here, a Jewish-Christian group there—were these writings kept alive. Rumors of their existence continued to circulate, as later writers could read the accounts of authors such as Irenaeus to see that once there had been a Gospel of Judas, which presented a nefarious and foolish alternative to the orthodox religion. But no one was particularly keen to find these writings or to preserve them for posterity. What would be the point? They contained falsehood and would simply lead people astray. Better to let them die an ignoble death.

And so they did. Only rarely were they copied. And eventually even these isolated copies disappeared, until modern times, when on very rare occasions one of them turns up, to show us anew that the orthodox understanding of religion was not the only one in the second Christian century. There was, in fact, a thriving opposition to this understanding, an opposition, for example, embodied in the recent gem of a discovery, the Gospel of Judas. Here is a book that turns the theology of traditional Christianity on its head and reverses everything we ever thought about the nature of true Christianity. For in this book the truth is not taught by the other disciples of Jesus and their proto-orthodox successors. These Christian leaders are blind to the truth, which was given only in secret revelations to the one disciple they had all agreed to despise—Judas Iscariot.

Judas alone, according to this hitherto lost view, knew the truth about Jesus. Jesus did not come from the creator of this world and was certainly not his son. He came from the realm of Barbelo, to reveal the secret mysteries that could bring salvation. It was not his death that brought this salvation. His death simply released him from this evil material world. For this world was not created by the one true God; it was the creation of inferior, lowly deities who were bloodthirsty rebels and fools. This material world is not a place to be embraced, it is not a realm that will be redeemed. It is a cesspool of pain, misery, and suffering, and our only hope of salvation is to forsake it. And some of us will do so. Some of us have a spark of the divine within, and when we die, we will burst forth from the prisons of our bodies and return to our heavenly home, the divine realm from which we descended and to which we will return, to live glorious and exalted lives forever.

THE GOSPEL OF JUDAS AND THE OTHER GOSPELS

Craig A. Evans

THE RESCUE, RESTORATION, AND PUBLICATION OF THE GOSPEL OF JUDAS constitute the ancient-manuscript highlight of the new millennium. Such discoveries are always celebrated by historians and scholars. Not surprisingly, the press release in April 2006 made headline news around the world. Overnight an ancient text became a modern best-seller.

What makes the discovery of the Gospel of Judas particularly interesting is that we had known of this writing since its mention by theologian and heresy-hunter Irenaeus in the late second century CE. He wrote of a "Gospel of Judas" in which Judas, of all people, had been entrusted with the mystery of the betrayal of Jesus. What could that have meant? Without the text itself, we would never know. Not a trace of it survived, not as a manuscript fragment nor even as a quotation in some ancient source.

A chance discovery in Egypt, perhaps in 1978, changed everything. Some 25 years later the Gospel of Judas was in the hands of scholars and now the public too has the opportunity to read this ancient text for themselves. What contribution will this new discovery make to our understanding of early Christian history? Does the Gospel of Judas shed new light on Judas and on his master Jesus of Nazareth? Will our understanding of the historical Jesus require revision? How exactly does the Gospel of Judas compare to the New Testament gospels (viz., Matthew, Mark, Luke, and John) and to other gospels outside the New Testament that have in recent years gained notoriety?

Readers who are not experts in the field may well get the impression from some recent publications that the New Testament gospels and several other gospels and gospel-like writings outside the New Testament were written at about the same time. Indeed, some scholars push the dates of the composition of the New Testament gospels as close to the end of the first century as possible and then argue for very early dates of some of the extra-canonical gospels (such as the Gospel of Thomas, the Gospel of Peter, the Secret Gospel of Mark, the Egerton Gospel fragment, and others). Although these moves are severely criticized in scholarly publications, they nevertheless persist in books and documentaries intended for popular consumption.

What readers need to know is that the question of the value of the extra-canonical gospels for research into the life and teaching of Jesus is very much a matter of debate among scholars. There are some who believe that a few of these writings may actually contain tradition as old as or older than what we have in the New Testament gospels. And, of course, there are many scholars who do not think this at all. The former therefore think research on the historical Jesus should take the extra-canonical sources into account, while the latter do not think the extra-canonical sources are of any significant help.

Before saying more about the extra-canonical gospels, further discussion of this issue of dates and chronology is probably necessary. Most readers have seen references to "first," "second," and "third" centuries. What is the significance of these dates? Jesus taught and ministered in the late 20s and early 30s of the first century. Paul wrote his letters in the late 40s to the early or mid-60s. Although it is debated, the Gospel of Mark was probably composed sometime in the mid- to late 60s and the Gospels of Matthew and Luke sometime after that (and some scholars in fact argue that Mark, Matthew, and Luke—also called the synoptic gospels—date to the 50s and 60s). The Gospel of John is usually dated to the early 90s. This means that most, perhaps even all, of the New Testament writings date to the first century. It also means the Gospel of Mark was written within one generation of the death of Jesus, which in all probability means that some people who had known Jesus were still living when this gospel was written and circulated.

Some think that the sayings source (or Q)—a collection of Jesus' teachings that Matthew and Luke used—dates to the 50s, perhaps even earlier. Accordingly, it is plausible to think that documents that date to the middle of the first century (such as Q and Mark) not only reach back to authentic sayings of and stories about Jesus, but these documents also would have been subject to critical assessment by living witnesses. It would not be easy for a gospel that misrepresents the life and teaching of Jesus to gain widespread acceptance in the middle of the first century, when many of Jesus' followers were still living and would be in a position to challenge distortions. This is why scholars who study the historical Jesus make frequent appeal to Q and the Gospel of Mark.

Not only do the earliest New Testament gospel sources date to the middle of the first century, the apostle Paul also refers to Jesus' teaching, to his words at the last supper, to his death and burial, and to his resurrection. This is very important, for Paul, who was converted to the Christian faith in the 30s, knew some of the original disciples and apostles, such as Peter, John, and James the brother of Jesus. Many of Paul's allusions to the Jesus tradition cohere, sometimes quite closely, with what we find in the New Testament gospels. This is what we should expect, if the New Testament gospels originated in the first century, utilizing oral and written sources in circulation in the lifetime of someone like Paul, whose mid-first-century writings we possess. For this reason most scholars of Christian origins believe that the New Testament writings provide us with our earliest and most reliable information about Jesus. This is why writings believed to have originated in the first century, especially in the middle of the first century, are widely accepted as our best sources for gaining information about the historical Jesus.

There are other reasons why major scholars concerned with the historical Jesus give priority to the New Testament gospels. One reason is that the historical, cultural, and political details found in the New Testament gospels, often mentioned only incidentally, can be confirmed by other sources (such as the writings of Josephus, the first-century Jewish historian) or by archaeology. The New Testament gospels talk about real places, real customs, real people, and real events—many of which can be confirmed by other sources. Moreover, the portrait of Jesus himself—as a teacher of disciples and as a public preacher and healer—is very consistent with what our sources tell us about Jewish teachers and healers. The way Jesus engages his critics and debates scripture is again true to what we know of first-century Jewish Palestine.

In the New Testament gospels Jesus comes across as a real person—not a talking head with no historical setting. In the New Testament gospels we read about real places, which in many cases archaeologists have excavated (such as Nazareth, Cana, Capernaum, and perhaps Bethsaida). The New Testament gospels aid historians and archaeologists in their work. The New Testament gospels provide important clues for reconstructing what happened or where something took place. None of this can be said for the gnostic gospels or other gospels and gospel-like writings from the second and third centuries. Indeed, the very form of the gnostic gospels—private, esoteric revelation—and the content of teachings attributed to Jesus—elaborate heavenly realms and deities—strongly warn against viewing these writings as being on par with the New Testament gospels.

Moreover, the New Testament gospels reflect the language of early Palestine. In them we encounter Hebrew and Aramaic words, usually transliterated and translated into Greek, the language in which the gospels themselves were written. Again, this is exactly what we should expect, if the New Testament gospels in fact preserve the words of an Aramaic-speaking teacher and his disciples. But this linguistic dimension is lacking in the second- and third-century gospels and gospel-like writings. The statements and actions of Jesus in the New Testament are credible and lifelike. Verisimilitude does not prove that Jesus really said this or did that, but it gives historians and critics confidence that they have access to potentially useful sources. In the later extra-canonical gospels and gospel-like writings, however, a lifelike Jesus is not to be found.

All of the gnostic gospels and extra-canonical sources date to the second century or later. Typical dates range from 140 to 160 CE. Some scholars argue for earlier dates, such as 120 to 140 (and some argue for later dates). Although it is theoretically possible that early, reliable information about Jesus—not found in the New Testament writings—could be preserved in some of these second-century writings, it is not too probable. This is why biblical scholars in the past have rarely appealed to writings such as the Gospel of Thomas, the Gospel of Peter, and the Gospel of Mary for additional information about Jesus. These writings are viewed as simply too late—written at least 100 years after the death of Jesus, or 50 to 80 years after the New Testament gospels were written.

In the scholarly and popular press of today, the most frequently mentioned writings outside of the New Testament are the Gospel of Thomas, the Gospel of Peter, the Egerton Gospel fragment (i.e., Egerton Papyrus 2), the Secret Gospel of Mark, the Gospel of Mary, and, of course, the recently restored and published Gospel of Judas. Most people have not heard of these writings until relatively recently, and often in connection with a book or television documentary, claiming to have discovered a Jesus "we have never known before." If these extra-canonical gospels were written long after the New Testament gospels, why do some scholars appeal to them? That is a good question, and this is where the discussion gets very interesting.

Some scholars have argued that *early editions* of the Gospel of Thomas and the Gospel of Peter reach back to the middle of the first century, that the Egerton gospel predates Mark and John—and indeed may have been on the writing table of the evangelist Mark himself—and that the Secret Gospel of Mark may represent an earlier form of the canonical Gospel of Mark. It is no wonder then—if these early dates and hypothetical early forms of these writings are valid—that some scholars make use of these extra-canonical sources in their reconstructions of the historical Jesus. Accordingly, the Jesus Seminar's assessment of the authentic words of Jesus came out under the title *The Five Gospels*, with the "fifth gospel" the Gospel of Thomas. What are we to make of all this? Is there really solid evidence that these writings outside the New Testament truly date—at least in some form—to the first century and contain sayings from and stories about Jesus that are early, independent, and perhaps even superior to what is found in Matthew, Mark, Luke, and John?

Until recently the extra-canonical gospels were not taken seriously as potential sources for Jesus research. Three-quarters of a century ago Rudolf Bultmann—who was by no means a conservative biblical scholar—regarded these gospels and related writings as nothing more than "legendary adaptations and expansions" of the canonical gospel tradition. Almost no one in his generation disagreed. Today the picture has changed, for some scholars dramatically, and for the general public very confusingly.

To put the Gospel of Judas in proper context it will be useful to review some of the better known and frequently mentioned extra-canonical gospels. We must ask just what these other gospels tell us and how the Gospel of Judas fits in with them.

GOSPEL OF THOMAS

Thirteen leather-bound books (or codices), written in the Coptic language, dating to about 350-380 CE, were found in Egypt sometime near the end of 1945 (near a place called Nag Hammadi). One of these books contains a writing that begins, "These are the secret words that the living Jesus spoke and Judas, even Thomas, wrote," and ends with the words, "the Gospel according to Thomas." Third- and fourth-century church fathers had mentioned a gospel that went by the name of the apostle Thomas. It seems, then, that the Gospel of

Thomas mentioned by Christian theologians 17 centuries ago had turned up in the dry sands of Egypt. This was a remarkable find, by any reckoning.

But there is more. When the new discovery was read and translated (and was found to contain a prologue and 114 sayings, or logia, mostly attributed to Jesus), scholars realized that parts of the Gospel of Thomas had in fact been found a half century earlier, in the 1890s, in a different part of Egypt, in a place called Oxyrhynchus. It turns out that three Greek papyrus fragments published at the turn of the century, numbered 1, 654, and 655, contain about 20 percent of the Gospel of Thomas, at least as compared with the Coptic version. The Greek fragments range in date from 200-300 CE.

The Gospel of Thomas is an esoteric writing, purporting to record the secret (or "hidden") teachings of Jesus, teachings reserved for those qualified to hear these teachings. I offer here a translation of the prologue and the first seven sayings, according to the Greek version (i.e., P. Oxy. 654), with restored letters and words placed in square brackets. We are able to complete most of the missing Greek text thanks to the fully preserved Coptic translation.

Prologue These are the [secret] words [that] the living Jesus [spo]ke a[nd Judas], even Thomas, [wrote].

§1 And he said, ["Whoever finds the interpretat]ion of these words will not taste [death]."

§2 [Jesus says], "Let him who se[eks] not cease [to seek until] he finds, and when he finds [he will be amazed; and when he is am]azed he will reign, an[d when he has reigned he will atta]in rest."

§3 Jesus says, ["If] those who lead you [say to you, 'Behold,] the kingdom is in the sk[y,' then] the birds of the sk[y will precede you. If they say th]at it is under the earth, then the fish of the se[a will enter it, preced]ing you. And the king[dom of God] is within you, [and it is outside of you. Whoever] knows [himself] will discover this. [And when you] know yourselves, [you will realize that] you are [sons] of the Father who l[ives. But if you will not] know yourselves, in [poverty you are] and you are pov[erty]."

§4 [Jesus says,] "A ma[n full of day]s will not hesitate to ask a ch[ild of seven day]s concerning the place of [life, and you will li]ve. For many who are fi[rst] will be [last and] the last will be first, and they [will become one and the same]."

§5 Jesus says, "K[now what is befo]re your sight, and [what is hidden] from you will be reveal[ed to you. For there is nothing] hidden which will not [become] reveal[ed], nor buried which [will not be raised]."

§6 [His disciples] q[ue]stion him [and s]ay, "How [shall we] fast, [and how shall we pr]ay, and how [shall we give alms]? What [diet] shall [we] observe?" Jesus says, "[Do not lie and what you ha]te, do not do; [for all things are revealed in the presence] of truth. [For nothing] hid[den will not become manifest]."

§7 "[. . . B]lessed is [the lion which man eats, and the li]on become[s man; and cursed is the man] whom [the lion eats . . .]."

The Jesus of the Gospel of Thomas is very, very different from the Jesus of the New Testament gospels. The private, esoteric orientation of the text is plainly evident. The opening line, "These are the secret words that the living Jesus spoke," should not be understood to imply that *all* of Jesus' teaching was secret (or hidden). Writings such as the Gospel of Thomas recognize and presuppose the public teachings of Jesus (as recorded, for example, in the New Testament gospels). What the Gospel of Thomas claims to record are the secret, or hidden words that Jesus spoke, *in private to Thomas and to his other disciples*. Thomas, of course, is the favored disciple, who understands Jesus more deeply than the other disciples and who is the one who writes the words of Jesus. The Jesus of the Gospel of Thomas urges his followers not to cease seeking until they find. They must know themselves, if what is hidden is to be revealed to them.

Although some scholars, such as Marvin Meyer, have argued that a version of the Gospel of Thomas may date to the first century, there are important factors that have led many scholars to conclude that Thomas is a late writing—not an early one: (1) Thomas is acquainted with at least half of the New Testament writings, which suggests composition no earlier than the middle of the second century. (2) Thomas contains gospel materials that scholars regard as late. (3) Thomas is familiar with later editing in the gospels. (4) Thomas shows familiarity with traditions distinctive to eastern, Syrian Christianity, traditions that did not emerge earlier than the middle of the second century (e.g., Tatian's *Diatessaron*). In light of this evidence, it is not surprising that many scholars do not see the Gospel of Thomas as an ancient source for the historical Jesus. Thomas may well contain some primitive tradition, but given its second-century Syrian affinities, heavy reliance on it is very risky.

GOSPEL OF PETER

Eusebius refers to the "writings that are put forward by heretics under the name of the apostles containing gospels such as those of Peter, and Thomas, and Matthias, and some others besides" (*Hist. Eccl.* 3.25.6). Still later Eusebius once again mentions the gospel attributed to Peter, this time in reference to Serapion, bishop of Antioch (in office 199-211). Initially the bishop allowed the Gospel of Peter to be read in his churches. After reading it and discovering heretical tendencies, the bishop ordered that it not be read.

In the winter of 1886-87, during excavations at Akhmîm in Egypt, a codex was found in the coffin of a ninth-century Christian monk. The manuscript comprises a fragment of a gospel, fragments of Greek Enoch, the Apocalypse of Peter, and, written on the inside of the back cover of the codex, an account of the martyrdom of the legendary St. Julian. The gospel fragment bears no name or hint of a title, for neither the beginning nor the conclusion of the work has survived. Because the apostle Peter appears in the text, narrating in the first person (v. 60, "But I, Simon Peter"), because it seemed to have a heretical, docetic orientation (that is, where the physical reality of Jesus appears discounted), and because the gospel fragment was in the company of the Apocalypse of Peter, it was widely assumed that the fragment belonged to the Gospel of Peter mentioned by Eusebius.

In recent years, the Akhmîm gospel fragment has enjoyed a resurgence of scholarly interest. Harvard professor Helmut Koester and some of his students have argued that it is indeed the Gospel of Peter and that it is not only independent of the New Testament gospels, but it may even be older. In a lengthy study that appeared in 1985, John Dominic Crossan argued that the Gospel of Peter, though admittedly in its final stages influenced by the New Testament gospel tradition, preserves a very old tradition, perhaps dating to the 40s or 50s, on which all four of the canonical gospels base their accounts of the Passion.

Many other gospel scholars, however, find these conclusions unconvincing, not least because of the presence of fantastic and obviously unhistorical elements. The author of the Akhmîm gospel fragment apparently possessed little accurate knowledge of Jewish customs and sensitivities. For instance, according to his version the Jewish elders and scribes camp out in the cemetery, as part of the guard keeping watch over the tomb of Jesus. Given Jewish views of corpse impurity, not to mention fear of cemeteries at night, the author of this fragment is unbelievably ignorant. Who could write such a story only twenty years after the death of Jesus? And if someone did at such an early time, can we really believe that the evangelist Matthew, who was surely Jewish and knew well Jewish sensitivities and traditions, would make use of such a poorly informed writing? One can scarcely credit this scenario.

Accordingly, can it be seriously maintained that the Akhmîm fragment's resurrection account, *complete with a talking cross and angels whose heads reach heaven*, constitutes the most primitive account? Is this the account that the New Testament gospel writers had before them? Or, is it not more prudent to conclude what we have here is still more evidence of the secondary, fanciful nature of this apocryphal writing? Does not the evidence suggest that the Akhmîm gospel fragment is little more than a blend of details from the four New Testament gospels, especially from Matthew, that has been embellished with pious imagination and apologetic concerns? Although theoretically Crossan's interpretation is possible, the evidence as a whole suggests that it is improbable.

There is yet another problem. Recently the identification of the Akhmîm gospel fragment with the Gospel of Peter mentioned by Eusebius has been called into question. The gospel fragment found in the ninth-century coffin may not be the Gospel of Peter at all, but a much later apocryphal gospel, loosely based on the New Testament. The fantastic details, such as the great height of the resurrected Jesus and the cross that accompanies him, reflects traditions in the second, third, and fourth centuries. Accordingly, this work gives every appearance of being late, not early. Anyone interested in learning more about the historical Jesus is well-advised to take this interesting source with a grain of salt.

THE EGERTON GOSPEL FRAGMENT

Egerton Papyrus 2 was found somewhere in Egypt and fell into the hands of scholars in 1934. It consists of four fragments. The fourth fragment yields nothing more than one illegible letter. The third fragment yields little more than a few scattered words. The first and second fragments offer four (or perhaps five) stories that parallel stories found in John and in the synoptic gospels (Matthew, Mark, and Luke). Köln Papyrus 255, discovered sometime later, constitutes a related fragment of the text. Some scholars have suggested that this gospel fragment, like the Akhmîm fragment discussed above, preserves old, pre–New Testament gospel tradition.

This view, however, faces a number of difficulties. First, several times editorial improvements introduced by Matthew and Luke in their respective retelling of Mark appear in Egerton (compare, for example, Egerton line 32 with Mark 1:40, Matthew 8:2, Luke 5:12, or Egerton lines 39-41 with Mark 1:44, Matthew 8:4, Luke 17:14). How can this be, if the Egerton fragment predates Mark? There are other indications that the Egerton papyrus is posterior to the New Testament gospels. The plural "kings" is probably secondary to the singular "Caesar" that is found in the synoptic gospels (and in Gospel of Thomas §100). The flattery, "what you do bears witness beyond all the prophets," may reflect John 1:34, 45 and is again reminiscent of later pious Christian embellishment that tended to exaggerate the respect that Jesus' contemporaries showed him (see the examples in Gospel of the Hebrews §2 and Josephus, *Antiquities* 18.3.3 §64).

Secondly, although Koester and others think it improbable that the author of the Egerton papyrus would have selected words and sentences from this and that New Testament gospel, is this not what Justin Martyr and his disciple Tatian did in the second century? Sometime in the 150s CE Justin Martyr composed a harmony of the synoptic gospels and some years later Tatian composed a harmony of all four New Testament gospels (i.e., the *Diatessaron*). If Justin Martyr and Tatian, writing in the second century, can compose their respective harmonies through the selection of sentences and phrases from this gospel and that gospel, why could not the author of the Egerton papyrus do the same thing? Indeed, it is probable that this is the very thing that he did do.

Third, the mixing of elements from the Gospel of John and the synoptic gospels is more easily explained as later conflation, rather than as early, pre–New Testament gospels tradition that has not yet bifurcated into the distinctive Johannine and synoptic streams of tradition, a proposal that strikes scholars as odd.

Not surprisingly, for these reasons and for others, not too many scholars who do historical Jesus research rely on the Egerton gospel fragment. They regard it as a second-century writing, in which elements of the New Testament gospels have been combined. Once again we may concede the possibility of the antiquity and perhaps priority of the Egerton gospel fragment, but the evidence taken as a whole tells against this possibility.

THE GOSPEL OF MARY

The Gospel of Mary, a fragmentary gnostic writing found in the Berlin Gnostic Codex, narrates a story in which Mary Magdalene relates to the disciples the private revelations that

Jesus gave her. Andrew and Peter express doubts that Mary is telling the truth, because her teaching is at variance with what they themselves had been taught. Mary weeps, saddened that they would think that she would misrepresent the words of the Savior. Levi rebukes Peter, defending Mary and exhorting the disciples to preach the gospel, "neither setting boundaries nor laying down laws, as the Savior said." The disciples then go forth and the Gospel of Mary comes to an end.

The purpose of the Gospel of Mary was to challenge those who "set boundaries" and "lay down laws" (10:13). Because Peter and Andrew reject Mary's teaching, we probably should infer that those who lay down laws appeal to the better-known apostles, whose teachings are preserved in the better-known, more widely circulated documents of the Christian communities. The group behind the Gospel of Mary is attempting to defend its teachings and, perhaps, the right of women to be teachers, perhaps in opposition to a growing institutionalization of Christianity and an increasing restrictiveness of the role of women (as perhaps seen in 1 and 2 Timothy, and Titus). This tension is also attested in the Gospel of Thomas, where Peter demands: "Make Mary leave us, for females are not worthy of (eternal) life" (§114). Jesus rebukes Peter, declaring that he will be able to transform Mary into a male, so that she and all other women thus transformed will gain entry into the kingdom of heaven.

In some recent writings, not least Dan Brown's phenomenal best-seller *The Da Vinci Code*, it has been speculated that Jesus and Mary were lovers, perhaps married and perhaps parents. Those who argue for this view appeal to the Gospel of Mary, where it says: "Sister, we know that you were much loved by the Savior, as no other woman" (6:1). The Gospel of Philip is also appealed to: "And the companion of the [Savior is] Mary Magdalene. [But Christ loved] her more than [all] the disciples [and used to] kiss her [often] on her [. . .]" (Nag Hammadi Codex II,3: 63,32-36). Some translations restore the text to read, "he used to kiss her often on her mouth," but that is pure conjecture. The author of this text may have imagined that Jesus kissed Mary often on the hand, forehead, or cheek. We do not know what the original text said; and, in any case, there is no warrant for assuming from these passages in the Gospel of Mary and the Gospel of Philip that Jesus and Mary were lovers. The texts do not say this, and there is no evidence from antiquity that anyone thought this.

The Gospel of Mary may well reflect struggles over church polity, the role of women, the issue of legalism in one form or another, and the limits of apostolic authority. But this writing, however it is to be understood, reflects a setting no earlier than the middle of the second century. We find in it nothing that can be traced with any confidence to the first century or traced back to the life and ministry of the historical Jesus and the historical Mary Magdalene.

THE SECRET GOSPEL OF MARK

At the annual Society of Biblical Literature meeting in New York in 1960, Morton Smith announced that during his sabbatical leave in 1958, at the Mar Saba Monastery in the Judean wilderness, he found the first part of a letter of Clement of Alexandria (circa 150-215) penned in Greek, in what was argued an eighteenth-century hand, in the back of a seventeenth-century edition of the letters of Ignatius. In 1973 Smith published two editions of his find, one learned and one popular. From the start, some scholars suspected that the text was a forgery and that Smith was himself the forger. Many scholars—including several members of the Jesus Seminar—have defended Smith and the authenticity of the Clementine letter.

What made the alleged find so controversial were two quotations of a mystical or secret version of the Gospel of Mark, quotations of passages not found in the public Gospel of Mark (that is, the version of Mark found in the Bible). In the first, longer passage, Jesus raises a dead man and then later, in the nude, instructs the young man in the mysteries of the kingdom of God. The homoerotic orientation of the story is hard to miss. This mystical version of Mark has since become known as the Secret Gospel of Mark.

Recently some very competent historians and experts in the detection of forgeries have suggested that the Clementine letter and the quotations of Secret Mark embedded within it constitute a modern hoax, and Morton Smith almost certainly is the hoaxer. Several scholars have for years suspected this to be the case, but the clear, recently published color photographs of the document have given experts in the science of the detection of forgeries the opportunity to analyze the handwriting of the document and compare it with samples of the handwriting of the late Professor Smith. Magnification of the handwritten text reveals the presence of what handwriting experts call the "forger's tremor." That is, the handwriting in question is not really *written*; it is *drawn,* in the forger's attempt to imitate a style of writing not his own. These tell-tale signs are everywhere present in the alleged Clementine letter. There are other tell-tale signs, such as spots of mildew, which indicate that the book spent its life in Europe or America, not in the arid Judean wilderness. Moreover, some of the distinctive themes in the document are in evidence in some of Smith's work published *before* the alleged find in 1958. Indeed, the whole story of the finding of a long-lost Greek document that could potentially embarrass the Christian church may well have been inspired by James Hunter's *The Mystery of Mar Saba*

(1940), in which a page of Greek text is discovered that apparently disproves the resurrection of Jesus. From evidence such as this it is now widely suspected that the Clementine letter, along with its quotations and discussion of a secret version of Mark, was penned by the late Professor Smith.

The extra-canonical gospels that have been briefly surveyed above are, with the obvious exception of Secret Mark, important works that need to be studied carefully. They tell us much about the second century and perhaps later centuries. But they do not tell us much, if anything, about the historical Jesus. The best sources for Jesus remain the New Testament gospels of Matthew, Mark, Luke, and John. This is so, not because they are part of the New Testament and not because they are "privileged," but because they are the oldest and most credible sources we have. Being the oldest and most credible sources explains why early Christians preferred them over the later, more eccentric gospels.

LOST CHRISTIANITIES

In recent years it has become quite fashionable to emphasize Christian diversity, suggesting that there were several very different expressions of Christian faith (or "Christianities") existing at the same time and that one of them just happened to win out. What eventually became "orthodoxy" triumphed over various other groups, including gnostics. The losing groups faded from history and their books of scripture disappeared. That Christian faith and its New Testament are what they are today is more or less an accident of history. So goes the argument.

Admittedly there is some truth to this scenario, but much of it is quite misleading and some of it is seriously anachronistic. As already mentioned, the New Testament gospels of Matthew, Mark, Luke, and John all originated in the first century, within a generation or so of the time of Jesus. The writings of the so-called "lost Christianities" were produced in the second and third centuries.

One aspect of the "Christianities" jargon that is misleading is the idea that *one particular version* of Christian faith won out, the version represented by the writings of the New Testament. The problem with this claim is that what we find in the New Testament is a diverse collection of writings. The contents of the New Testament are not monolithic, but represent a range of views. The four gospels are not identical in perspective. In Mark's gospel Jesus as the true son of God is set in contrast to Rome's faith placed in the emperor as the son of God and beginning of good news. In Matthew's gospel Jesus fulfills the Jewish Law and Prophets and teaches his disciples the way of righteousness. In Luke's gospel Jesus is Savior and Benefactor of the whole human race. In John's gospel Jesus is the incarnation of God's divine Logos. In his letters Paul emphasizes the saving grace to be found in the good news of the resurrection of Jesus, arguing against the need to keep the Law of Moses. A very different perspective is found in the letters of James and Hebrews. Still more views are expressed in the Johannine and Petrine letters.

The point is that the Christian faith that survived was itself quite diverse. What "won out," if such language is even appropriate, were expressions of Christian faith that had credible links to Jesus and his disciples. The "lost Christianities," of which some scholars speak, in reality were groups that emerged in the second and third centuries, groups that adopted elements of Christian teaching. Among these were gnostics, who rejected the Old Testament perspective of God and creation, transforming Jesus into a revealer who enters the world in disguise and teaches an elite following how to escape. Another was Marcion, who wanted to purge Christian faith and Christian scripture of Judaism. And there were others. Exactly how "Christian" these groups and individuals truly were is a matter of debate. None of them reflects the actual teachings of Jesus himself and his disciples, who embraced the faith and scriptures of Israel.

The Gospel of Judas is one of these interesting second-century writings that take a very dim view of the faith of Israel and its scripture. To this writing we now turn.

GOSPEL OF JUDAS

The Gospel of Judas makes a meaningful contribution to our understanding of second-century Christianity and the diverse groups that laid claim to the story of Jesus and his disciples. In Judas we apparently have a very early exemplar of Sethian gnosticism, a form of gnosticism that may have roots in Jewish pessimism that emerged in the aftermath of the disastrous wars in 66-70 and 115-117 CE.

Exactly how we should understand the disciple Judas in the Gospel of Judas is very much an open question. Initially many of us thought the much maligned disciple of the Christian tradition is portrayed as a hero of sorts, the one disciple who truly understood Jesus and who faithfully carried out his wishes. But other scholars have weighed in, among them April DeConick, Louis Painchaud, Birger Pearson, Gesine Schenke Robinson, and John D. Turner, challenging this line of interpretation by suggesting that the Judas of the Gospel of Judas is no hero. This is an impressive list of capable scholars of Coptic gnosticism, whose views should be taken very seriously. This interesting debate is addressed in this book in the essay by Gesine Schenke Robinson.

However we understand the portrayal of Judas, it is highly unlikely that the Gospel of Judas preserves for us authentic, independent material, material that supplements our knowledge of Judas and his relationship to Jesus. No doubt some popular writers will produce some fanciful stories about the "true story"—about who Judas really was and what he really did—but that is all that they will produce—fanciful stories.

One thing that the Gospel of Judas has made me wonder about is the interesting statement we find in the Gospel of John, where Jesus says to Judas, "What you are going to do, do quickly" (John 13:27). The other disciples do not understand what Jesus has said, imagining that he meant one thing or another (John 13:28-29).

What is interesting is that we have at least two other instances where Jesus evidently made a private arrangement with a few disciples, about which other disciples did not know. We see this in the securing of the animal for Jesus' entry into Jerusalem (Mark 11) and in the finding of the upper room, where Jesus and his disciples might eat supper (Mark 14). Exegetes and historians may rightly wonder if the episode in John 13 is a third instance, in which Jesus had a private arrangement with a disciple, an arrangement that was not known to the others. It could be that, as the disciples speculated, Jesus was sending Judas to accomplish some task, perhaps relating to Jesus' security later that evening. If so, then Judas' appearance in the company of armed men, who seize Jesus and deliver him to the ruling priests, was a betrayal indeed.

It may be that we have in the Gospel of Judas a greatly developed, tendentious, unhistorical, and imaginative expansion of this theme: Yes, Jesus had a private understanding with Judas, and yes, Judas handed Jesus over to his enemies. But was it a betrayal, or was it all part of Jesus' plan? And even if it was Jesus' plan, in what light does the Gospel of Judas place Judas? No doubt this question will continue to be hotly debated.

Of course, whatever arrangement the historical Jesus may have had with Judas (and John does seem to be a witness that he may have had some sort of arrangement), being handed over to the ruling priests was certainly not what Jesus planned. Accordingly, the Gospel of Judas, however it should be understood, may provide us with a clue that will lead us to ask new questions about why Judas betrayed Jesus and exactly how he did so.

Writings outside the New Testament and even later than the New Testament sometimes offer important assistance in going about the task of New Testament interpretation. The Gospel of Judas does not provide us with an account of what the historical Judas really did or what the historical Jesus really taught this disciple, but it may preserve an element of tradition—however greatly developed and embellished—that could serve exegetes and historians, as we struggle to understand better this enigmatic disciple. No doubt scholars will disagree among themselves over how early we should date the Gospel of Judas and exactly what it tells us, but all will agree that this is an important ancient text.

The Gospel of Judas is one more early writing from the first centuries of the Christian movement. As such, it is of great importance and warrants careful study. From it we will learn more about the diverse portraits of Jesus that circulated in the second century and forced the Christian church to think through what it believed.

JUDAS AND THE GNOSTIC CONNECTION

Marvin Meyer

IN THE LATTER PART OF THE SECOND CENTURY, IRENAEUS OF LYON, writing in his tract *Against Heresies,* mentions the Gospel of Judas, and he doesn't like it much. He reports that the people behind the Gospel of Judas claimed that Judas Iscariot knew the ways of God and that Judas was the only one of the disciples who understood the truth. Judas consequently performed the mystery of the betrayal, the handing over of Jesus, Irenaeus continues in his report, and this act is linked to the dissolution of all that is earthly and heavenly. Irenaeus suggests that these are the very ideas found in the Gospel of Judas, and his description fits rather well with the contents of the recovered text of the Gospel of Judas from Codex Tchacos.

Irenaeus denounces the Gospel of Judas as a wicked fabrication of people he calls "gnostics," *gnōstikoi,* a Greek word that means "knowers" or "people of knowledge." Although some scholars criticize the word *gnostic* as too broad of an umbrella term, covering many different types of beliefs, Irenaeus says that certain religious people referred to themselves as "gnostics." The knowledge claimed by these people is not worldly knowledge but mystical knowledge, knowledge of God and self and the relationship between God and self.

In the Gospel of Judas, the word *gnōsis* is used twice (50, 54), and in the second instance the text mentions "knowledge to be [given] to Adam and those with him, so that the kings of chaos and the underworld might not lord it over them." This passage suggests that the knowledge bestowed upon Adam and the descendants of Adam—the human race—offers protection and salvation from the powers of this world. As Bart D. Ehrman also points out in his essay, the Gospel of Judas and Jesus himself in this gospel proclaim salvation through knowledge, the self-knowledge of the divine light within a person.

The gnostics discussed by Irenaeus and others constitute a major school of mystical religious thought throughout antiquity. Today scholars commonly refer to the students of that school of thought as Sethian gnostics. When we refer to gnostics in a more general way, we extend the use of that term to include those groups that are related to Sethian gnostics. Several of the Nag Hammadi texts are part of this Sethian gnostic school, with the Secret Book of John regarded as the classic text of Sethian thought. The Gospel of Judas may also reflect this Sethian school, representing an early, second-century form of Christian Sethian thought.

The central confession of Judas Iscariot, the leading disciple in the Gospel of Judas, places the gospel in the Sethian gnostic tradition. In the gospel, the other disciples misunderstand who Jesus is and claim him to be the son of their God, the God of this world, but Judas declares to Jesus: "I know who you are and where you have come from. You have come from the immortal aeon of Barbelo. And I am not worthy to utter the name of the one who has sent you" (Gospel of Judas 35). The phrase "the immortal aeon (or eternal realm) of Barbelo" is a familiar phrase in Sethian texts. It indicates the exalted realm of the divine beyond this world, and it is associated with the divine figure Barbelo, who is a prominent character in Sethian writings, where she often assumes the role of our Mother in heaven.

The origin of Barbelo and her name remains obscure, but it may come from the ineffable four-letter name of God, YHWH, or Yahweh—Jehovah in Elizabethan English—used in the Jewish Scriptures and within Judaism. The Hebrew word for "four," *arba,* may designate the holy name, and the name of Barbelo may derive from Hebrew for an expression like "God (compare *El*) in (*b-*) four (*arb*(*a*))," that is, God as known through the ineffable name.

In the extant Gospel of Judas, the figure of Barbelo is not expanded into a character in a mythic drama, as in other Sethian texts, and the precise identity of Barbelo remains uncertain. It is not clear whether she is the divine Mother. Nor is Barbelo mentioned in the account of the appearance of Autogenes, the Self-Generated, later in the gospel (47). Barbelo is mentioned only once in the Gospel of Judas, by Judas himself, and his affirmation of the ineffability of the divine name may recall the holiness of this name within the Jewish heritage. Judas professes that Jesus is from the divine, and he does not take the name of the divine in vain.

Whatever the precise meaning of the name, Barbelo becomes the divine originator of light and life and the source—often the Mother—of the divine Child in Sethian texts. If Jesus is from the immortal realm of Barbelo, as Judas confesses in the Gospel of Judas, then he is also a divine being from the realm above.

John D. Turner, a scholar who has specialized in the study of the Sethians, gives a convenient summary of the most significant cosmological figures of Sethian thought:

> Many Sethian treatises locate at the summit of the hierarchy a
> supreme triad of Father, Mother, and Child. The members of this

triad are the Invisible Spirit, Barbelo, and the divine Autogenes. The Invisible Spirit seems to transcend even the realm of being itself, which properly begins with Barbelo as his projected self-reflection. The Child is self-generated (*autogenēs*) from Barbelo either spontaneously or from a spark of the Father's light, and is responsible for the ordering of the remainder of the transcendent realm, which is structured around the Four Luminaries and their associated aeons. The realm of becoming below this usually originates from Sophia's attempt to instantiate her own contemplation of the Invisible Spirit all by herself and without its permission; in many accounts, this act produces her misshapen offspring the Archon as the maker of the phenomenal world.

Sethian texts frequently portray the world we inhabit with features drawn from their interpretation of Adam and Eve, which are used to tell a remarkable and revolutionary story. The creator of the world, according to Sethians, is actually a megalomaniacal demiurge, but human beings are exalted above the creator and his powers by virtue of the spark of divinity within them. If people come to know their true divine selves, they will be able to escape the clutches of the powers of this world and realize the peace of enlightenment.

In the Gospel of Judas, Jesus reveals to Judas what he and readers of the text need to know in order to achieve a proper understanding of who Jesus is and what life in the world and beyond entails. The Sethian perspective of the Gospel of Judas is representative of early Sethian thought, but at the same time Sethian themes of the gospel do not seem fully developed. The Gospel of Judas, I propose, may thus provide a glimpse of Sethian gnostics in the process of developing their version of the good news of Jesus.

THE GREAT ONE, BARBELO,
AND AUTOGENES THE SELF-GENERATED

The Gospel of Judas proclaims its cosmological message about the divine and the nature of the divine in a typically Sethian way. Barbelo is mentioned, as are the Father and Autogenes the Self-Generated. The Father or Parent of All is identified as "the great invisible Spirit" in one passage within the extant pages of the Gospel of Judas (47), as he is in many Sethian texts, and he is also described in a number of additional places throughout the Gospel of Judas as the Spirit—and as "the Great One" (53). It appears to be inappropriate to speak of the Great One as "God," or "divine," in the Gospel of Judas. That term seems to be reserved for lower powers of the universe and for the creator of this world, for "all those called 'divine'" (48). In the Gospel of Judas, the Great One seems to transcend the finite term God. The same theological point is made in the Secret Book of John:

> The One is a sovereign that has nothing over it. It is God and Parent, Father of All, the invisible one that is over All, that is incorruptible, that is pure light at which no eye can gaze. The One is the invisible Spirit. We should not think of it as a God or like a God. For it is greater than a God, because it has nothing over it and no lord above it. It does not [exist] within anything inferior [to it, since everything] exists within it, [for it established] itself. (Nag Hammadi Codex II:2-3)

The transcendence of the Great One is emphasized in the Gospel of Judas. When Jesus reveals the secrets of the universe to Judas, he uses phrases to depict the transcendent one that recall the language of 1 Corinthians 2:9, the Gospel of Thomas 17, the Prayer of the Apostle Paul in the Nag Hammadi library, and other texts. Jesus says:

[Come], that I may teach you about the [(things) . . .] that [no (?)] human will (ever) see. For there exists a great and boundless aeon, whose extent no generation of angels could (?) see, [in] which is the great invisible Spirit, which no eye of an [angel] has ever seen, no thought of the heart has ever comprehended, and it was never called by any name. (47)

Other Sethian texts, especially the Secret Book of John and Allogenes the Stranger, present fuller descriptions of the transcendence of the divine. In the Secret Book of John, the revealer says:

The One is
illimitable, since there is nothing before it to limit it,
unfathomable, since there is nothing before it to fathom it,
immeasurable, since there was nothing before it to measure it,
invisible, since nothing has seen it,
eternal, since it exists eternally,
unutterable, since nothing could comprehend it to utter it,
unnamable, since there is nothing before it to give it a name.

The One is the immeasurable light, pure, holy, immaculate.
It is unutterable, and is perfect in incorruptibility. Not that it is
just perfection, or blessedness, or divinity: It is much greater.

The One is not corporeal and it is not incorporeal.
The One is not large and it is not small.
It is impossible to say, How much is it? What [kind is it]?
For no one can understand it. (II:3)

This description reminds us again of the words of Judas to Jesus near the beginning of the Gospel of Judas: "I am not worthy to utter the name of the one who has sent you" (35).

Autogenes the Self-Generated is discussed in the Gospel of Judas 47-50, when Jesus reveals the glorious manner in which the divine extends itself and comes to full expression. The Great One, the great invisible Spirit, transcends all aspects of this world of mortality here below, so some manifestation of the divine must bring about the creation and salvation of the world. That manifestation is Autogenes the Self-Generated. Jesus states that from a luminous heavenly cloud, showing the brilliance of the divine, comes a divine voice calling for an angel, and from the cloud Autogenes the Self-Generated appears. Autogenes is a term commonly used in Sethian texts to characterize the offspring of Barbelo and the term underscores the independence of the Child. The Child, as Autogenes, is a self-starter. The name Autogenes, or "Self-Generated," works particularly well in the Gospel of Judas, where the Self-Generated simply emerges, by himself, from the heavenly cloud after the voice calls out.

Elsewhere in Sethian literature, the account of the appearance of the Child Autogenes can become more complicated, and in the longer version of the Secret Book of John, the appearance of the Child is portrayed in such a way as to suggest an act of spiritual intercourse between the transcendent Father and Barbelo the Mother:

> The Father gazed into Barbelo, with the pure light surrounding the invisible Spirit, and his radiance. Barbelo conceived from him, and he produced a spark of light similar to the blessed light but not as great. This was the only Child of the Mother-Father that had come forth, the only offspring, the only Child of the Father, the pure light. The invisible virgin Spirit rejoiced over the light that was produced, that came forth from the first power of the Spirit's Forethought, who is Barbelo. (II:6)

In the Gospel of Judas, Jesus goes on to recount how four other angels, or messengers, elsewhere called "luminaries," come into being through the Self-Generated, and they serve as attendants for the Self-Generated (47). In other Sethian stories, the Four Luminaries are assigned names: Harmozel, Oroiael, Daveithai, and Eleleth. Increasing numbers of angels and aeons—heavenly beings—come into existence, "[myriads] without number," according to the Gospel of Judas, as the brilliance of the divine is expressed. Eventually the expansion of the divine extends to the aeons, luminaries, heavens, and firmaments of the universe, and their numbers correspond to features of the world, especially units of time. There are twelve aeons, like the number of months in a year. There are 72 heavens and luminaries, like the traditional number of nations in the world according to Jewish lore. There are 360 firmaments, like the number of days in the solar year (less the five intercalary days). The number 24 is also used, as the number of hours in a day (Gospel of Judas 49-50).

This section of the Gospel of Judas is so closely paralleled by passages in the text Eugnostos the Blessed and a related text, the Wisdom of Jesus Christ, that I believe some sort of textual relationship is possible. The author of Eugnostos the Blessed describes the production of aeons and other powers in two relevant passages:

> The twelve powers I have discussed came together with each other, and each produced <6> males and <6> females, for a total of 72 powers. Each of the 72 in turn produced 5 spiritual powers, bringing the number to 360 powers. They are united in will. In this way immortal humanity came to symbolize our realm. The first one to conceive, the son of immortal humanity, functions as a symbol of time. The [savior] symbolizes [the year]. The 12 powers are

symbols of the 12 months. The 360 powers who derive from the savior stand for the 360 days of the year. And the angels who came from them and who are without number stand for the hours and minutes. (Nag Hammadi Codex III:83-84)

Some of these, in dwellings and chariots, were in ineffable glory and could not be sent into any creature, and they produced for themselves hosts of angels, myriads without number, to serve and glorify them, as well as virgin spirits and ineffable lights. They are free of sickness and weakness. There is only will, and it comes to expression at once. (Nag Hammadi Codex III:88-89)

In the Gospel of Judas, these theological reflections, intricate and complex as they are, disclose a sophisticated way of thinking about the divine. In the beginning, it is said, there is the infinite, unnamable, ineffable deity—if we may even call the Great One a "deity" or, for that matter, use any finite word whatsoever to describe the One. The Great One expands through aeons and countless entities to a fullness of divine glory that shines down toward our world below. Were it not for a tragic mistake in the divine realm, a lapse of wisdom, all would have remained glorious. But, many Sethian texts declare, a lapse did occur.

CORRUPTIBLE WISDOM AND THE CREATOR

According to Sethian texts, there was a fall from grace at the beginning of time that precipitated an event of cosmic proportions. In the Bible, Genesis 3 narrates the story of Adam and Eve yielding to the will of the serpent and eating from the tree of the knowledge of good and evil, against the will of God. Sethian texts often speak of divine wisdom, Wisdom personified as Sophia, who shares traits with Eve and falls into an error that has grave consequences. The surviving portion of the Gospel of Judas doesn't include the story of Sophia and the fall of Sophia. There is only a single reference to wisdom in a fragmentary part of the text, where, with little explanation, she—or it—is called "corruptible wisdom" (44). Following a gap, there is a reference to "the hand that has created mortal people," which may link wisdom to the God who creates this world.

In the Secret Book of John, the account of the fall of Wisdom is presented in some detail:

> Now Sophia, who is the Wisdom of Insight and who constitutes an aeon, conceived of a thought from herself, with the conception of the invisible Spirit and Foreknowledge. She wanted to bring forth something like herself, without the consent of the Spirit, who had not given approval, without her partner and without his consideration. The male did not give approval. She did not find her partner, and she considered this without the Spirit's consent and without the knowledge of her partner. Nonetheless, she gave birth. And because of the invincible power within her, her thought was not an idle thought. Something came out of her that was imperfect and different in appearance from her, for she had produced it without her partner. It did not resemble its mother, and was misshapen. (II:9-10)

In the Letter of Peter to Philip, the revealer in the text provides a further crucial detail of the fall of Mother Sophia. In the Codex Tchacos version of the letter, the revealer says:

> To begin with, [concerning] the deficiency of the aeons, what is deficient is disobedience. The Mother, showing poor judgment, came to expression without the command of the Great One. He is

the one who wished, from the beginning, to set up aeons. But when she [spoke], the Arrogant One appeared. A body part from within her was left behind, and the Arrogant One grabbed it, and deficiency came to be. This, then, is the deficiency of the aeons. (3-4)

The word "deficiency" is a key word in Sethian and other gnostic texts, and it may also occur in Gospel of Judas 39, though in that text the Coptic word may be translated as either "sacrifice" or "deficiency." (We have opted here for the former translation as the preferred one.) The deficiency, or diminution in the divine light, comes from a bad conception, according to the Secret Book of John, and from disobedience and poor judgment, according to the Letter of Peter to Philip. The Mother of the Letter of Peter to Philip could be either Sophia or Eve, and considering the connection between Sophia and Eve in gnostic literature, the ambiguity may be deliberate. As the story of Sophia unfolds in the literature, part of the divine spirit passes from Sophia to her child, the creator of this world, who eventually blows it—right into humanity (Genesis 2:7). Thus, Sophia's loss means that human beings have the light of the divine within themselves.

This may be the larger story of "corruptible wisdom" in the Gospel of Judas. All that is deficient in the world of the divine and the world below stems from the lapse of Wisdom, and when the light within people becomes one with the divine again, then Sophia is restored and the fullness of the divine is realized. Something of that bliss may be experienced now, gnostic texts suggest, but the final experience of divine wholeness occurs when people leave their mortal bodies. In the Gospel of Judas, Jesus says that when people of the generation of Seth—gnostics—pass away, their physical bodies die but their souls remain alive and return, liberated, to their heavenly home (43). At death, all that belongs to the body and is at home in this mortal world is to be relinquished. The mortal bodies of people of knowledge are to be surrendered, Jesus says to Judas, so that "their souls go up to the aeons on high" (44).

The account of wisdom in the Gospel of Judas, however, may well be a variant of this story. In the long cosmogonic account that dominates much of the Gospel of Judas (47-53), neither wisdom nor Sophia are mentioned, and she can hardly be hiding in a lacuna, because there is no lacuna big enough to accommodate her and her sad story. Theoretically the reference to El (compare Eleleth?) at the very top of page 51, with some lacunae following, could make a brisk reference to a fall from grace, since Eleleth, the fourth luminary, plays a role in the production of the lower, mortal realm in such Sethian texts as the Holy Book of the Great Invisible Spirit and Three Forms of First Thought. Or, instead of an actual fall of Wisdom or rupture in the divine in the Gospel of Judas, perhaps the text means to describe a gradual devolution or diminution of the divine light as it comes to expression in this world. Such a career for the light of God in this world might call to mind aspects of the flowing forth of the divine light in Jewish mystical traditions—for example, at a later time, in Jewish Kabbalah, with the tree of life and the Sefirot, the channels of divine energy emanating from the infinite God, Ein Sof. Or again, the place commonly reserved for Sophia in gnostic texts may be taken by Judas himself, whose life as described in the Gospel of Judas may mirror the life of Wisdom, and of any gnostic who represents the light of God trapped in this world—a proposal we shall explore later in this essay.

In some gnostic traditions, particularly Valentinian traditions, two figures of Wisdom are mentioned, higher Wisdom and lower Wisdom, probably in an effort to deal with the delicate issue of how to affirm the supreme goodness of the divine and still acknowledge the reality of evil in a flawed world.

This issue, the question of theodicy or the problem of evil, remains one of the most difficult and significant of issues in theological discussions to the present day. What is evil, and where does it come from? Is God somehow involved in evil? In the Valentinian Gospel of Philip, higher Wisdom is called Sophia or Echamoth, lower Wisdom Echmoth, "the Wisdom of death" (Nag Hammadi Codex II:60), and the higher Wisdom of God is shielded from the evil of this mortal world. Similarly, perhaps, the Holy Book of the Great Invisible Spirit also makes mention of "Sophia of matter" (Nag Hammadi Codex III:57). How the reference to "corruptible wisdom" in the Gospel of Judas relates to the more fully developed ways of construing Wisdom in gnostic texts remains uncertain.

What is clear is that wisdom is "corruptible." The offspring of Sophia and the product of her mistake, described as a misshapen child in the Secret Book of John and dubbed "the Arrogant One" in the Letter of Peter to Philip, is the chief ruler and the creator of the mortal world, well-known from Sethian texts. In the Gospel of Judas and other gnostic traditions, the creator of this world is not a kind and gentle figure. As creator and demiurge, he is responsible for keeping the divine light of wisdom imprisoned within mortal bodies. In Gospel of Judas 51, the creator is named Nebro and Yaldabaoth, and another, Saklas, collaborates with him. Forms of all three names are known from other Sethian sources. Yaldabaoth may mean "child of chaos"; Saklas means "fool." The name Nebroel or Nebruel occurs in the Holy Book of the Great Invisible Spirit and Manichaean sources; in the Gospel of Judas, the name Nebro is spelled without the honorific suffix -el (meaning "God" in Hebrew). In the Holy Book, Nebruel seems to be a demoness who has sex with Sakla and gives birth to 12 aeons (III:57).

Jesus in the Gospel of Judas uses graphic language to tell Judas what the creator of this world looks like, and he is not a handsome guy. Jesus says, "Look, from the cloud there appeared an [angel] whose face flashed with fire and whose appearance was defiled with blood" (51). When his face flashes with fire, he looks like Yaldabaoth in the Secret Book of John (II:10), and when he is defiled with blood, he looks like Sophia of matter in the Holy Book of the Great Invisible Spirit (III:56-57).

According to the Gospel of Judas, the creator and his cronies create this world below with rulers, angels, and powers all around. The institution of the bureaucracy of angelic powers is portrayed in a passage that is somewhat damaged:

"The twelve rulers spoke with the twelve angels: 'Let each of you [. . .] and let them [. . .] generation [. . . five] angels': The first is [Se]th, who is called 'the Christ.' The [second] is Harmathoth, who is [. . .]. The [third] is Galila. The fourth is Yobel. The fifth is Adonaios. These are the five who ruled over the underworld, and first of all (or, the first ones) over chaos." (51-52)

Parallels to this passage are found in the Secret Book of John (II:10-11) and the Holy Book of the Great Invisible Spirit (III:58), and these parallels depict the same sort of bureaucracy of rulers of the world as the Gospel of Judas, albeit in a more full-blown way. The Holy Book reads:

Through the will of the Self-Generated, [Sakla] the great angel said, "There shall be . . . seven in number. . . ." He said to the

[great angels], "Go, [each] of you reign over your own [world]."
And each [of these] twelve [angels] left. [The first] angel is Athoth,
whom [the great] generations of people call . . . , the second is
Harmas, [the eye of fire], the third [is Galila], the fourth is Yobel,
[the fifth is] Adonaios, who is [called] Sabaoth, the sixth [is Cain,
whom] the [great generations of] people call the sun, the [sev-
enth is Abel], the eighth, Akiressina, the [ninth, Youbel], the tenth
is Harmoupiael, the eleventh is Archir-Adonin, the twelfth [is
Belias]. These are set over Hades [and chaos].

The Secret Book of John states that seven powers are
placed over the seven spheres of heaven (for the sun, moon,
Mercury, Venus, Mars, Jupiter, and Saturn) and five over the
depths of the abyss.

The presence of "[Se]th, who is called 'the Christ,'" as a designation of the first angel in the list of five angels in the Gospel
of Judas, and Harmathoth as the peculiar name assigned to the
second angel, may give reason to pause. Several creative ways of
reading the names in the text at this point have been proposed
by scholars, as the notes to the translation indicate. It may be
most probable that here an author or editor of the text sought
to offer a modest Christian addition to a cosmogonic revelation
that otherwise is entirely Jewish, and inserted—awkwardly, in
a way that does not cohere well with the role of Seth or Christ
in other Sethian texts—"[Se]th, who is called 'the Christ.'" But
that left two traditional angelic names, Athoth and Harmas,
and only one angelic spot, so that the names were combined in
the text. Thus the angel Harmathoth was born.

The bureaucrats of this world are in place in the Gospel
of Judas, and this abyss of a world—the cosmos, "corruption"
according to Gospel of Judas 50—is ready to be occupied. All
it needs is a family of tenants.

SETH AND THE CREATION OF ADAM AND EVE

The figure of Seth, the third son of Adam and Eve, is a significant figure in the Gospel of Judas. The Gospel of Judas lists Seth (also called Christ) as a curiously positioned angelic ruler of the world, as we have seen, and it refers to "the generation of Seth" (also called "the great generation," "that generation," and the generation "with no ruler over it") and the parents of Seth, Adam and Eve, as well as Adamas, described as heavenly Adam in a cloud of light. What does all of this mean? In the Bible, the first family is highly dysfunctional: The parents get into trouble with God and are evicted from their garden home, and the first two boys, Cain and Abel, both come to bad ends. According to Genesis 4-5, Adam and Eve bore another son named Seth, "another seed" produced in the image of Adam just as Adam was produced in the image of God. He is the one who carries on the family of Adam. Further, Genesis reports that Seth himself has a son, Enoch, and at that time people begin to call upon the Lord Yahweh with his holy name.

Apparently, because Seth is "another seed," he inherits the epithet Allogenes, which means "one of another kind" or "stranger" in Greek. There is a Sethian text in Nag Hammadi Codex XI, which I already mentioned, entitled Allogenes, or Allogenes the Stranger, and Porphyry the Neoplatonic author cites a "revelation of Allogenes" that may be this very text from the Nag Hammadi library (*Life of Plotinus* 16). Moreover, Epiphanius refers to multiple books of Allogenes (or Allogeneis, in the plural; *Panarion* 39.5.1).

A fragment of the book identified as the fourth tractate of Codex Tchacos, immediately after the Gospel of Judas, has been given the provisional title Book of Allogenes on account of the main character within the text. We might wonder whether this text could be one of the other books of Allogenes.

In the last extant tractate of Codex Tchacos, as in other Christian Sethian texts, Allogenes takes on the role of Jesus. In the text, Jesus is Seth the Stranger incarnated as the Christian savior, and in the person of Allogenes he faces temptations by Satan and experiences transfiguration in a luminous cloud, just as Judas (or Jesus) may be transfigured in a luminous cloud in the Gospel of Judas (57-58).

Sethian texts are typically articulated with interests derived from the Platonic philosophical world, and in keeping with these interests, Adam in the Gospel of Judas is both an ideal figure of humanity above as well as an earthly figure below. Adam, called Adamas (probably a pun on the Greek word *adamas,* "steel-like," "unbreakable"), "was in the first cloud of light that no angel could (?) (ever) see among all those called 'divine'" (48). A little later reference is made to "the incorruptible [generation] of Seth" (49). While in the Gospel of Judas Seth is not explicitly placed with Adamas in the divine realms, as in other Sethian texts, Jesus states near the end of the text that "prior to heaven, earth, and the angels, that generation (the generation of Seth), which is from the aeons, exists" (57). Such a statement of the exalted place of origin of the generation of Seth may imply that Seth himself is also assumed to be an exalted figure in the divine realms in the Gospel of Judas.

The Secret Book of John gives a more detailed account. According to this text, heavenly Adamas resides in the first aeon with the first luminary Harmozel, in a manner reminiscent of the heavenly home of Adamas in the Gospel of Judas, and Seth resides in the second aeon with the second luminary Oroiael (II:9). The seed of Seth also dwells in heaven, as in the Gospel of Judas. According to the Secret Book of John, the seed of Seth is in the third aeon with the third luminary Daveithai, and heavenly Adam is named

Pigeradamas (or Geradamas)—"Adam the stranger," "holy Adam," or "old Adam."

The fact that heavenly Adamas is said in the Gospel of Judas to be in the first luminous cloud means that he dwells in the glory of the divine, close to the Great One. This close connection between Adamas, ideal humanity, and the Great One confirms what was suggested by scholar Hans-Martin Schenke. Schenke saw a close link between the supreme deity in gnostic thought and the archetypal human, so that, in different ways and with different patterns, transcendent humanity comes to be associated with the transcendent One. This connection between God and Man in Sethian texts is exemplified in the primal revelation of the divine in Sethian texts, where the divine voice rings out from above, "Humanity exists, and the child of humanity" (or, "Man exists, and the son of man"; Secret Book of John II:14).

The story of the creation of earthly Adam and Eve and their children in the Gospel of Judas, concise as it is, is told with biblical and Platonic themes: "Then Saklas said to his angels, 'Let us create a human being after the likeness and after the image'" (52). This follows the account of Genesis and interprets it in Platonic and gnostic terms. Genesis 1:26 states that the creator makes humanity after the image and likeness of the divine, and in Sethian traditions this is interpreted to mean that earthly Adam is patterned after the ideal image of heavenly Adamas. This gnostic idea of a ruler of the earth creating human beings here below after the image and in the form of the transcendent human in the heavenly realm above is similar to the Platonic belief that the demiurge creates the world on the basis of forms and ideas from the realm of ideas.

Other gnostic texts, including Sethian texts, offer similar reflections upon Genesis 1:26. The Letter of Peter to Philip has Jesus describe the creative work of the Arrogant One as the production of "an image instead of an [image], a form instead of a form" (4). In the Secret Book of John, the account is much more developed, and it distinguishes between creation in the image of the divine and creation in the likeness of the archons and authorities of the world:

> A voice called from the exalted heavenly realm, "Humanity exists, and the child of humanity." The first ruler, Yaldabaoth, heard the voice and thought it had come from his mother. He did not realize its source. The holy perfect Mother-Father, the complete Forethought, the image of the invisible One, being the Father of All, through whom everything came into being, the first human— this is the one who showed them and appeared in human shape. The entire realm of the first ruler quaked, and the foundations of the abyss shook. The bottomside of the waters above the material world was lit up by this image that had appeared. When all the authorities and the first ruler stared at this appearance, they saw the whole bottomside as it was lit up. And through the light they saw the shape of the image in the water. Yaldabaoth said to the authorities with him, "Come, let us create a human being after the image of God and with a likeness to ourselves, so that this human image may give us light." They created through their respective powers, according to the features that were given. Each of the authorities contributed a psychical feature corresponding to the figure of the image they had seen. They created a being like the perfect first human, and said, "Let us call it Adam, that its name may give us power of light." (II:14-15)

One of the distinctive features of the Gospel of Judas is its emphasis upon astronomical and astrological concerns, particularly the role of the stars and planets in human life, and this emphasis likewise seems to be based upon Platonic themes. Other Sethian texts also comment on the ways in which the powers of the sky rule over people, but the Gospel of Judas says that a person is given a soul and is guided by a star. In the Gospel of Judas, Jesus tells Judas that people have souls, but only the people of the generation of Seth have souls that are immortal: "The souls of every human generation will die. When these people, however, have completed the time of the kingdom and the spirit leaves them, their bodies will die, but their souls will be alive, and they will be taken up" (43).

Here and elsewhere in the text, the spirit of a person may be contrasted with the soul. The spirit may be the breath of life, while the soul may be the inner person who comes from the divine and returns to the divine. The same contrast helps to explain what Jesus means when he teaches Judas, in Gospel of Judas 53, that although ordinary people have spirits in them for a period of time, people of the generation of Seth have both spirits and souls from the Great One. Jesus also reflects upon the stars, and in Gospel of Judas 42, Jesus remarks to Judas and the other disciples, "Each of you has his own star."

The interest in souls and stars recalls Plato's statements on souls, stars, and the creation of the world. In the *Timaeus,* Plato has Timaeus cite a statement by the creator of the world, and then Timaeus comments on how souls are assigned to stars:

> Thus the creator spoke, and once more into the cup in which he had previously mingled the soul of the universe he poured the remains of the elements and mingled them in much the same manner; they were not, however, pure as before, but diluted to the second and third degree. And having made it, he divided the whole mixture into souls equal in number to the stars, and assigned each soul to a star; and having there placed them as in a chariot, he

showed them the nature of the universe, and declared to them the laws of destiny, according to which their first birth would be one and the same for all—no one should suffer a disadvantage at his hands; they were to be sown in the instruments of time severally adapted to them, and to come forth the most religious of animals; and as human nature was of two kinds, the superior race would here after be called humanity. . . . The person who lived well during his appointed time was to return and dwell in his native star, and there he would have a blessed and congenial existence. (41d-42b; trans. Benjamin Jowett; slightly revised by the author.)

The native star of Judas is singled out for special mention through what Jesus tells him near the end of the Gospel of Judas. Judas may be destined for grief, as he is warned throughout the text. He will become the thirteenth one, the outcast from the circle of the twelve disciples, cursed by others and replaced in the circle of the twelve by another (Gospel of Judas 35-36; Acts 1:15-26). Jesus calls Judas the thirteenth "daimon" (44), a term that is used by Plato for the guiding spirit of Socrates and is employed in Middle Platonic, Neoplatonic, Hermetic, and magical literature in a neutral or even positive way for intermediary beings. However, this term also designates evil demons and unclean spirits in much of Jewish and Christian literature. In one way of reading the text, Jesus promises, in spite of all the suffering and opposition faced by Judas, that the future will bring blessing and joy. Jesus tells Judas to look up and recognize that among all the stars above, his star leads the way (57).

By the middle of the third century, Sethian texts that incorporated these sorts of Platonic themes and numerous concepts from Middle Platonism and Neoplatonism were in circulation, and some of them were discussed and critiqued by the Neoplatonic philosopher Plotinus and the students in his philosophical school in Rome. These Platonizing Sethian texts read in Rome may include tractates from the Nag Hammadi library, such as Allogenes the Stranger, as we have seen. One of the complaints of the Platonists against the gnostics and their texts was that they were too hard on the demiurge—Nebro, Yaldabaoth, Saklas—and they portrayed him in too negative a fashion. It is true that Sethian texts have little good to say about the creator of this world, and to that extent Sethians may have been out of step with other Platonists. Nonetheless, it is evident that Sethian texts, including the Gospel of Judas, embraced themes derived from Plato, and in their own way they worked them into their understanding of the divine and the universe.

JUDAS ISCARIOT IN THE GOSPEL OF JUDAS

Judas Iscariot plays a central role throughout the Gospel of Judas, and he is the chief recipient of the revelatory knowledge imparted by Jesus on the nature of God and the character of the cosmos. On the one hand, of the disciples Judas alone knows Jesus and professes who he is, and many complimentary things are said about him. Yet it is also stated in the text that he, the "thirteenth daimon," is subjected to suffering and persecution and may be prevented from ascending on high—though one day he (or his star) will rule over the "thirteenth aeon." These apparent discrepancies in the evaluation of Judas in the Gospel have caused some scholars to conclude that Judas is not a good figure after all. Rather he is a tragic figure, even a demonic figure. Consequently, some scholars believe that the Gospel of Judas proclaims a message permeated with tragedy and even parody. True, someday Judas may rule over the thirteenth aeon, but the thirteenth aeon may be considered to be the abode of the demiurge Yaldabaoth. So, according to the Gospel of Judas, Judas may be destined to join the demiurge and reside with him in his unpleasant realm. Sethian texts like the Holy Book of the Great Invisible Spirit and Zostrianos make occasional mention of the thirteen aeons and the God (the demiurge) of the thirteen aeons, and the Revelation of Adam highlights thirteen kingdoms, though in a fairly vague way. Conversely, another Sethian text from the Nag Hammadi library, Marsanes, discusses the "thirteenth seal" as the dwelling place of "the unknown silent one," the highest God, in a different context. None of these texts, though, refers specifically to the expression "thirteenth aeon," a key phrase for understanding Judas in the Gospel of Judas.

The phrase "thirteenth aeon" does occur elsewhere in gnostic literature, in texts that have been known for a very long time. The phrase "thirteenth aeon" shows up more than forty times in the Pistis Sophia (and is also found in the Books of Jeu), where it is "the place of righteousness" located above the twelve aeons and the heavenly home of the twenty-four luminaries—including Sophia, who calls the thirteenth aeon "my dwelling place." In the literature of antiquity and late antiquity, the thirteenth realm can occupy a place just above the twelve (who are often considered to be the signs of the zodiac), on the border of the infinite—a somewhat ambiguous place, as in the Pistis Sophia, between the world of mortality below and the world of the divine on high. According to the Pistis Sophia's version of the myth, Sophia, straining to ascend to the light above, is deceived and comes down from the thirteenth aeon, descending through the twelve aeons to chaos below. Here in this world she is oppressed, and the powers of the world, including lion-faced Yaldabaoth, seek to rob her of the light within her. For a while, she is prevented from leaving the place of her oppression. In the words of Pistis Sophia herself, the cohorts of Authades, the arrogant one, have behaved harshly:

> They have surrounded me, and have rejoiced over me, and they have oppressed me greatly, without my knowing; and they have run away, they have left me, and they have not been merciful to me. They turned again and tempted me, and they oppressed me with great oppression; they gnashed their teeth at me, wanting to take away my light from me completely.

In the midst of her suffering, Pistis Sophia—the wisdom of God weakened and languishing in this world, reflective of the soul of the gnostic trapped here below—cries for salvation, and eventually her cry is heard:

> Now at this time, save me, that I may rejoice, because I want (or, love) the thirteenth aeon, the place of righteousness. And I will say at all times, May the light of Jeu, your angel, give more light. And my tongue will sing praises to you in your knowledge, all my time in the thirteenth aeon. (1.50)

In other words, Sophia comes from the thirteenth realm above; she is separated from—and separated for—that realm, to use the language of the Gospel of Judas; and she is destined to return there again. While here below, moreover, she refers to herself with another term that resonates with Judas' portrayal in the Gospel of Judas: as a daimon. In her fourth repentance, Sophia bemoans her fate: "I have become like a peculiar demon (*daimōn*), which dwells in matter, in whom is no light. And I have become like a spirit counterpart (*antimimon ᶜmpn(eum)a*) which is in a material body, in which there is no light-power" (1.39).

Again, in her twelfth repentance, Sophia laments: "They have taken away my light and my power, and my power is shaken within me, and I have not been able to stand upright in their midst, I have become like matter which has fallen; I have been cast on this side and that, like a demon which is in the air" (1.55). The word used for 'demon' here is *refsoor*, the Coptic equivalent of the Greek *daimonion*.

Hence, in a manner that closely parallels the portrayal of Judas Iscariot in the Gospel of Judas, Sophia in the Pistis Sophia is likened to a daimon, perhaps as an intermediary being. She is persecuted at the hands of the archons of the twelve aeons, and though long separated from it, she will return to her dwelling place in "the thirteenth aeon, the place of righteousness." That is the good news of Sophia in the Pistis Sophia.

It turns out that just this sort of link between Judas and Sophia, or Wisdom, apparently was made by gnostics already in the second century, as Irenaeus of Lyon informs us. According to Irenaeus in *Against Heresies,* certain Valentinian gnostics, who must have been enunciating their beliefs around the same time in the second century when the Gospel of Judas was being composed and read, established a close connection between the suffering of Sophia and the passion of Judas—both being linked, says Irenaeus, to the number twelve, with Judas numbered as the twelfth and final disciple in the circle of the twelve and Sophia numbered as the twelfth aeon.

Irenaeus argues against the Valentinian gnostics as follows, from his proto-orthodox perspective:

> Then, again, as to their assertion that the passion of the twelfth aeon was proved through the conduct of Judas, how is it possible that Judas can be compared with this aeon as being an emblem of her—he who was expelled from the number of the twelve, and

never restored to his place? For that aeon, whose type they declare Judas to be, after being separated from her Enthymesis (thought, reflection), was restored or recalled to her former position; but Judas was deprived of his office, and cast out, while Matthias was ordained in his place, according to what is written, "And his bishopric let another take" (Acts 1:20). They ought therefore to maintain that the twelfth aeon was cast out of the Pleroma (the heavenly fullness of the divine), and that another was produced, or sent forth to fill her place; if, that is to say, she is pointed at in Judas. Moreover, they tell us that it was the aeon herself who suffered, but Judas was the betrayer, and not the sufferer. (Maybe Irenaeus did not read the Gospel of Judas on the sufferings of Judas.) Even they themselves acknowledge that it was the suffering Christ, and not Judas, who came to the endurance of passion. How, then, could Judas, the betrayer of him who had to suffer for our salvation, be the type and image of that aeon who suffered? (2.20)

So Irenaeus—who at least knew of the existence of a text called the Gospel of Judas—admits that in the second century there were gnostics who compared Judas and Wisdom and were convinced that Judas was "the type and image of that aeon who suffered." (Incidentally, he also states, just prior to his reference to the Gospel of Judas, that some gnostics declared that after the resurrection, Christ, who himself was linked to Sophia, ascended to the right hand of Yaldabaoth for a thoroughly positive purpose—to aid in the salvation of souls.) This admission of Irenaeus, combined with the close similarities in theme and terminology in the presentations of Judas and wisdom in the Gospel of Judas and the Pistis Sophia (and the Books of Jeu), may allow us to draw a fascinating conclusion regarding the role of Judas Iscariot in the Gospel of Judas.

I suggest that among certain gnostics of the second century, including some Valentinians and the folks who wrote
and used the Gospel of Judas, the figure of Judas may well be
presented in terms that are reminiscent of the figure of Wisdom, and that the account of Judas in the Gospel of Judas may
be read with elements of the fall, passion, grief, and redemption of the wisdom of God in mind. Like Sophia in other texts
and traditions, Judas in the Gospel of Judas is separated from
the divine realms above, even though he knows and professes
the mysteries of the divine and the origin of the savior; he
goes through grief and persecution as a daimon confined to
this world below; he is enlightened with revelations that no
human will ever see; and at last he is said to be on his way,
much like Sophia, to the thirteenth aeon of gnostic lore.

The story of Judas, like the story of Sophia, recalls the
story of the soul of any gnostic who is in this world and longs
for transcendence. The Gospel of Judas may be understood
to portray Judas as the type and image of wisdom and of the
gnostic, and the text proclaims how salvation may be realized—not, it is emphasized, through a theology of the cross
and the experience of sacrifice but through gnosis and insight
into the nature of the divine and the presence of the divine in
the inner lives of people of knowledge.

Without a doubt this interpretation of the Gospel of Judas
calls into question many of the central tenets of an argument
for the text to be viewed as a tragedy and Judas to be nothing
more than a tragic disciple. Still, a number of uncertainties of
interpretation inevitably will linger as long as the lacunae on
the top portion of pages 55-58 of the Gospel of Judas, with
the account of the conclusion of the story of Jesus and Judas,
are unresolved. Furthermore, there certainly is room for a
more nuanced approach of the text, one that takes seriously

the diverse features of this challenging document. I suspect that in the future the figure of Judas Iscariot in the Gospel of Judas may be interpreted, in the light of such parallel texts as those cited here, as neither a completely positive character nor a totally demonic being, but rather a figure, like Sophia, and like any gnostic, who is embroiled in this world of mortality yet is striving for gnosis and enlightenment. To this extent there is room for aspects of a revisionist interpretation to be joined to a more positive interpretation of the Gospel of Judas, to give a balanced approach to the text. After all, Judas, like Wisdom, is caught between the worlds of mortality and immortality, looking for liberation, and the Gospel of Judas shows how liberation may be achieved. Thus, the evidence of the Gospel of Judas, together with insights drawn from the Pistis Sophia, the Books of Jeu, and Irenaeus of Lyon, may provide a new set of perspectives on Judas and Wisdom in second-century gnostic literature.

THE GOSPEL OF JUDAS AS A CHRISTIAN SETHIAN TEXT

The Gospel of Judas appears to be an early Christian Sethian gospel with teachings of Jesus presented to Judas Iscariot, to announce a way of salvation and enlightenment based upon knowledge of self and the divine. The message of the Gospel of Judas is that, just as Jesus is a spiritual being who has come from above and will return to glory, so also the true followers of Jesus are people of soul, whose being and destiny are with the divine. Already those who know themselves can live in the strength of the inner person, the "perfect human" mentioned by Jesus in his comments to the disciples (35). At the end of their mortal lives, people who belong to that great generation of Seth will abandon everything of this mortal world, in order to free the inner person and liberate the soul.

The gospel's teachings are those of Jesus the Christian savior, and the story recounts the betrayal of Jesus, yet the major instruction given by Jesus about cosmology and the secret things of the universe (Gospel of Judas 47-53) contains very little that could be considered specifically Christian. This cosmological account is based on innovative Jewish concepts and interpretations of Jewish Scripture and is influenced by Platonic ideas; the only indisputably Christian element in the entire account is the brisk and unusual reference to "[Se]th, who is called 'the Christ'" (Gospel of Judas 52). The cosmological account thus seems to have had its origin in an earlier Jewish Sethian context, and it has been taken over and lightly Christianized as the teaching of Jesus. In other words, Jewish Sethian teaching is transformed into Christian Sethian teaching in the Gospel of Judas. Such a transformation is also evident elsewhere in gnostic literature. The Secret Book of John is another Sethian text that seems to have been composed as a Jewish gnostic document and lightly Christianized into the teaching and revelation of Jesus. Similarly, Eugnostos the Blessed is a Jewish gnostic text, in the form of a letter, that has been edited and expanded into the teachings of Jesus in dialogue with his disciples, in the Wisdom of Jesus Christ.

Jesus, then, is understood to be the teacher and revealer of knowledge in the Gospel of Judas. He is from the divine and will return to the divine, and he gives instruction to Judas and members of the generation of Seth. In other Sethian Christian texts, Jesus takes on a similar role, and commonly he is associated with Barbelo, Autogenes the Self-Generated, and Seth. In the Secret Book of John, Christ is identified with the Self-Generated and becomes the son of divine Barbelo (II:6-7). In the Holy Book of the Great Invisible Spirit, Seth is clothed with "the living Jesus," and Jesus becomes the incarnation of

Seth. In the Book of Allogenes from Codex Tchacos, Jesus is presented as Allogenes the Stranger, a form of Seth. In the Three Forms of First Thought, the Logos or Word, with links to Seth, announces that it has put on Jesus and has carried him from the cursed wood (Nag Hammadi Codex XIII,50). Jesus in the Gospel of Judas is also associated with Barbelo, but the nature of their relationship is unclear, and how Jesus relates to Autogenes the Self-Generated, if at all, is unknown. The only explicit connection between Jesus and Seth in the Gospel of Judas is in that list of the angelic figures who rule over chaos and the underworld.

Questions remain about figures of Jesus and Judas according to the Gospel of Judas, but not about the proclamation of Jesus to Judas—and to the readers of the text. Jesus proclaims a mystical message of hope and freedom, articulated in Sethian gnostic terms. He leaves Judas and the readers of the gospel with a word of enlightenment and liberation. It is clear that the mystical message of the Gospel of Judas, and of Jesus in the Gospel of Judas, however it may be nuanced, remains supremely good news—from a gnostic point of view, the very best news in the world. In the end, gnosis—and wisdom—triumph.

JUDAS, A HERO OR A VILLAIN?

Gesine Schenke Robinson

WHEN THE HYPE CALMS DOWN, THE SERIOUS SCHOLARSHIP CAN BEGIN.
This is the way it has happened with almost every archaeological discovery relating to the New Testament. We may
recall the sensations about the Gospel of Mary, the Gospel of
Thomas, the Gospel of the Savior, ossuaries with names allegedly connected to Jesus, and the like. The initial excitement
about the Gospel of Judas was no exception. It was followed
by the publication of a preliminary translation prepared by an
editorial team, to which the scholarly community is indebted
for their meticulous work in restoring the manuscript that
was so badly damaged and for taking the risk of making it
accessible in the shortest time possible.

It soon became clear, however, that the Gospel of Judas had
captivated the imagination of the first editors to a much greater
extent than the text itself supports. With the gradual availabil-
ity of transcriptions of the restored text and images, it became
possible to check the provisional translation against the actual
Coptic wording and to reevaluate the overall assessment of
this manuscript. Mistakes have been acknowledged, and the
translation in some places amended, but the widely spread
misconception is harder to correct, and the sensationalized

reading is still promulgated and passed on from publication to publication. Since the translation is so essential for the understanding of the meaning of the text, in the end notes I will provide quotations from my own translation where it differs in significant ways from the one given in this book.

In order to appreciate the Gospel of Judas and the role of Judas in it, two levels of representation must be taken into account: one in the New Testament environment and the other in the gnostic environment. Both levels are sometimes so utterly intertwined that it is easy to lose sight of which perspective is required at what level. Since the Gospel of Judas is a gnostic text, everything said and done by any character involved has to be interpreted in a gnostic way, not seen through a New Testament lens. The Jesus we find there is not the person of the gospels we are familiar with, simply having a different relationship with Judas from the one the gospel writers convey. Nor is Judas an ideal disciple and Jesus' most trusted friend, who only did what Jesus asked and who received the ultimate reward, his ascent on high. Jesus certainly does not need anyone to free him from his mortal coil, as he demonstrates within the text by appearing and disappearing like the Jesus of the canonical gospels in his postresurrection appearances. Though the connection of Judas Iscariot with the term *gospel* may be intriguing, the text shows no interest in vindicating Judas, no matter how much we would like to repair the relationship between Judaism and Christianity by eradicating the bad rap Judas was commonly given, using his portrayal as the traitor to justify spilling Jewish blood in revenging his deed for centuries.

The Gospel of Judas is full of irony and probably contains hidden coded words that the original audience would easily have understood but that we laboriously have to unearth by way of accurate translation and erudite interpretation. For instance, we will detect, in due course, that the stars stand for destiny, the kingdom for the archontic realm, and the disciples for the leaders of the orthodox church from the time of the document. In terms of genre, the text presents itself as a revelatory dialogue in which Jesus answers questions of his disciples, interprets their visions, and teaches them about the everlasting generation, the cosmic order, and the stars that govern human affairs. Yet he seems to have bestowed his revelations on them to no avail, since now, at the end of his journey on earth, his disciples are still ignorant, and he stands on the other side of almost every issue they hold dear. He mocks them and laughs a great deal about their lack of understanding. For them, the gospel offers little hope, since nobody seems to be able to escape from the clutches of this world. Jesus will render a devastating eschatological verdict over human generations, who will be devoured in the final dissolution of the entire cosmos. The "good news" is meant solely for the *implied* audience—the Christian-gnostic community lying behind the Gospel of Judas. They could confidently feel excluded from this ultimate destiny. Yet in order to determine the specific role Judas plays in all this, we have to attend more closely to the details of the story as it unfolds.

The opening sentence of the Gospel of Judas includes a peculiar chronological notation, according to which Jesus conveyed his message "during eight days, three days before his passion." With the phrase "before his passion," the text stays vaguely within the New Testament environment, alluding to the crucifixion, but turns it on its head in an ironic twist by hinting at what will only be revealed at the end: The spiritual Jesus had already left this world *before* his mortal counterpart is handed over. Hence, the communication took place on eight sequential days shortly before Passover, ending with the departure of the true Jesus three days before, according to gnostic belief, only an empty body that carried him during his earthly journey is crucified. In some gnostic texts, the spiritual Jesus even stands by and laughs about the ignorance of those supposedly tormenting him. In addition to already exposing the fallacy of the orthodox church, a theme that becomes more and more apparent during the course of the account, the introductory verses also define the message itself in a specific way. The initial phrase, "The secret *declaration of judgment* that Jesus communicated to Judas Iscariot," seems to express precisely what Jesus is about to impart. Not only will he render a final verdict on the church and its leaders, but also Judas will receive a revelation of his own demise. Thus, the primary phrase provides the proper definition of the message to be delivered and ties it to the overall eschatological theme prevalent throughout the composition.

Following the incipit, both the initial and the concluding scenes of the Gospel of Judas sound like a summary of settings familiar from the canonical gospels. A résumé of his ministry introduces Jesus as having performed signs and wonders, and upon calling the twelve disciples, he reveals to *them* (not just to Judas) the secrets surrounding the world and its end. Concluding the document, the anonymous narrator returns to the New Testament environment, depicting a truncated version of the scene we know as Judas' betrayal. The mortal Jesus prays as Jewish authorities wait for an occasion to detain him. Finally, Judas assists in the plot and receives money in return. The scene is abbreviated because it no longer has any real function. What happens between Jesus' departure and the crucifixion of the corporeal body that carried him becomes extraneous.

Within this framework the account unfurls. When Jesus first encounters his disciples, he laughs about their ignorance. They believe that their devotion and pious practices are what is required of a good Christian. Ironically, they believe that the God they are worshiping is Jesus' Father. How utterly wrong they are! Only one disciple knows who Jesus *really* is, and this one is Judas. Upon Jesus' questioning as to whether these ignorant worshipers would even know him, only Judas dares to respond and utters his now renowned confession. He admits to knowing that Jesus was sent to them from the transcendent realm. Is he then not the best of all disciples, since he is the one most knowledgeable about Jesus? Yet, more importantly, *how* does he know about Jesus' true origin prior to the upcoming revelation? In the canonical gospels, especially the Gospel of Mark (see, for example, Mark 3:11, 5:7), nobody *knows* who Jesus really is except the demons. Does Judas know because he also is a demon? Jesus will later call him a demon and, with his challenge, may even have tricked the demon in Judas into this acknowledgment.

Yet, given that Judas is portrayed as just another clueless disciple throughout the text, the designation as demon should not be overinterpreted, especially since Jesus uses this term teasingly within a play on words; its negative connotation presumably alludes more to Judas' subsequent "betrayal" than to familiar demonology. Moreover, the confession originally may have simply intended to counteract Peter's confession in the New Testament (in Mark 8:27-30, Jesus calls Peter "Satan"; in John 6:66-69, following Peter's confession, Judas is characterized as a devil) and merely consisted of the first part, "I know who you are and from where you have come," only to be extended at a time when the Sethian unit later in the text was adopted.

Why is Jesus then granting Judas a revelation? Here the irony is on full display: Since Jesus recognizes that Judas is aiming much higher, he mockingly promises to tell him the "mysteries of the kingdom." Judas may enter this kingdom one day but will be very aggrieved when he gets there (35,21-27). The irony lies in the deception, a seeming promise immediately followed by a put-down. For the "kingdom" is not the exalted place to which Judas aspires, but rather the demonic world of the inferior demiurge and creator God called Saklas, whom Judas and the other disciples serve. It is not the higher realm of the holy generation about which Judas hopes to hear (36,6-9). Just as Eleleth sets the boasting demiurge straight when he claims to be the only God with nobody besides him, Jesus sets Judas straight by making clear that the realm of "that genera-tion" is completely out of his reach (37,1-10). Jesus knows that Judas will suffer when he realizes what the "kingdom" actually is. Here we have a play on the words "kingdom" and "*that* generation." For throughout the text, "that generation" always refers to the transcendent realm that is great, holy, and *without* a king (53,24)—a place reserved for the holy, which no one connected to the cosmos would ever see. Much of the confusion and resulting misinterpretation in the preliminary edition of the Gospel of Judas may have come from not clearly separating these sometimes intentionally ambiguous terms.

Judas' gloomy prospect becomes even more obvious after he recounts his vision and begs Jesus to take him along into what is apparently Jesus' heavenly dwelling place. Jesus bluntly tells him that his star misled him into thinking he could some day enter the upper realm of the universe (45,8-13). Having called him the thirteenth demon, irony again comes into play. The stage is set for another play on words, this time on the word "thirteenth" here and elsewhere in the text. The allusion to the future selection of another disciple as replacement for Judas (Acts 1:21-26) is only one side of the story; Judas was already told this part of his lot in life. Yet the "thirteenth" also designates the highest place above the twelve aeons of the archontic kingdom. Jesus uses this play on words to mockingly point to Judas' ultimate destiny: As the *thirteenth* demon he will only be able to reach the *thirteenth* aeon (46,19–47,1). Even though he will reign over this kingdom, whose inhabitants will curse him, the promotion is not all that high compared to what he is denied. Judas had already realized his curtailed fortune when he anxiously asks whether it could be true that he and his descendants would only preside over the archons. Jesus ironically seems to comfort him again, only to warn him another time that he will be very much aggrieved when he gets there. Judas did not gain anything for having received this revelation. He understood already what was implied when Jesus told him about the erroneous stars that control everyone's fate. There was nothing more to be done. He is predestined by his star to be stuck in the thirteenth aeon, just as is his star itself (55,10-11). No matter how hard he tries, he will end up ruling over the archons, angels, and stars, the powers holding sway over the world, not even close to the honorific position that was ascribed to him by the initial interpretations of the Gospel of Judas.

Although Jesus conveys his message mainly to Judas, there is no indication that the other disciples were not also present. When the dialogue is resumed after a large cosmological discourse, Jesus clearly talks to all of them again, even though Judas keeps asking the questions. There the topic of the revelation about the holy generation and the stars in relation to humans is also resumed. Jesus laughs at the erroneous stars, because even though they control all human generations, together with their creator they will be annihilated in the cosmic destruction. Mentioned here is also the perishable Sophia, but on par with the demiurge, not with Judas. She is by no means the "Wisdom of God," an epithet reserved for the divine consort of the supreme God; it can never be applied to the renowned "fallen Sophia." The condition and state of confusion in which the corruptible Sophia finds herself in other gnostic texts, her "fall, passion, grief, and redemption," neither compares to the portrayal of Judas in the document at hand, nor would Judas' standing change if there were a link between the two figures, since according to the Gospel of Judas, neither of them will see the holy generation.

After having delivered his final revelation, Jesus once more turns to Judas and points to a cloud full of light and a star surrounded by other stars. Judas is told that his star leads the way (57,15-20). This was supposed to confirm Judas' leading role above and beyond the role of the other disciples. Yet here again, Jesus deals with Judas in utter irony. After all we have learned about Judas and his future prospect, as well as about the errant stars, Judas' star can only lead the other stars into bringing about the apocalyptic destruction, not exactly something to brag about.

The narrator tells us that Judas "looked up and saw the luminous cloud." Then the sentence either continues or a new sentence begins, starting with "He entered it." Since there is no clear antecedent, this pronoun can refer back to either Judas or to Jesus. It is hardly conceivable, however, that Judas would ascend and then immediately reappear in order to betray Jesus in the next scene. The gnostic Jesus, on the other hand, does freely ascend to his divine realm and reappears at will throughout the text. Moreover, the following sentence clearly alludes to the voice from the cloud in the transfiguration of Jesus (see Mark 9:7, Matthew 17:5, and Luke 9:34-35). In the same way Judas, like everybody else, hears the voice from the cloud, but it is Jesus who enters it. This is surely also an allusion to the New Testament, where the cloud lifts Jesus up and carries him into heaven (see Luke 24:5 and Acts 1:9), even though in the Gospel of Judas this event takes place before the betrayal and crucifixion. After Jesus fulfills his task of delivering his message, a cloud from the world of light lifts him up and takes him home. Judas cannot follow him, as Jesus told him before; he has to fulfill his own destiny. Hence, in the brief concluding narrative, Judas conforms to the wish of the Jewish authorities. Yet it is clear that the man about to be handed over is not the same Jesus; he is not named by the narrator again but simply referred to as he. It is now only the empty body that gave Jesus his human appearance on earth.

The revelatory dialogue outlined thus far could have been the document that once caught the eye of Irenaeus. In his brief summary, he gives a rather mild assessment of the Gospel of Judas. However, the manuscript we now possess contains two other sections that do not seem to fit Irenaeus' appraisal. One is a vision report by the disciples, the other the cosmological unit. The vision report charges the orthodox church and its leaders so severely that it would certainly have roused Irenaeus' ire. The disciples saw a large house with an altar to which *twelve* priests brought offerings, watched by an approving crowd. The people participating in the sacrificial ritual were accused of all sorts of wicked, lawless, and evil deeds, including human sacrifice (38,14-23), which were apparently done by orthodox Christians baptized in Jesus' name. Jesus tells his disciples that they were to blame and throws in their face what they have done. The apostles themselves are the twelve priests, and their followers in the orthodox church are the cattle unwittingly sacrificed to a God they do not know is deficient

(39,18–40,1). He sharply rejects sacrificing and unmistakably commands them to stop this fruitless exploit, because the offerings only benefit the God of the Hebrew Scriptures, who is the evil archon Saklas, to whom these orthodox Christians already are lost.

When the topic is resumed toward the end of the text, Jesus tells Judas that he will exceed all of those who offer sacrifices. Yet again, in an ironic twist, the praise becomes a mockery. Far from Judas performing the greatest service imaginable by liberating Jesus from his mortal body, he is willing to offer Saklas the greatest sacrifice: Jesus himself. Thus, Judas will beat all others in doing something evil rather than beneficial. That he will not succeed, but merely deliver an empty body, transforms him into a *tragic* hero. Yet the prediction that Judas will only hand over "the man who carries" Jesus further proves that the separation of the spiritual and the corporeal part of Jesus happened *before* Judas could execute his plan—and thus Jesus disappeared into the cloud, not Judas.

It is obvious that the concept of sacrifice has no positive connotation in this text. The Christian-gnostic sect using the Gospel of Judas may have perceived the orthodox church as continuing only thinly veiled the old ways of the failed Jewish religious practices, exemplified by the temple cult with its sacrificial rituals. The polemic also shows that they reject the christological interpretation of Jesus' death as sacrifice necessary for salvation. Moreover, the mention of sacrificing wives and children could indicate that the gnostic sect despised the readiness for martyrdom, preached as necessity and widely accepted in orthodox Christianity, as a pointless sacrifice to a mediocre god, who himself will be destroyed together with his creation. There is no hope of salvation for anyone in this sacrificial approach, not even with the sacrifice of Jesus.

In view of this heresy and its severe refutation of Christian religious practices, Irenaeus would certainly not have kept quiet. He would surely have ranted much louder against a group that exhibited such callous and unforgiving language. From fornication to baby killing, there is no immorality too heinous to be used as slander of the church's leaders and to malign the worshipers of the God of the Hebrew Scriptures. This kind of polemic was usually employed against the *opponents* of the church—and precisely by heresy hunters like Irenaeus. We may infer, therefore, that the Gospel of Judas we now possess comprises much more material than the one on which Irenaeus reported. The text may have been subjected to various editorial modifications and textual adaptations in the course of its long history of transmission. After all, almost two hundred years lie between the original Greek version and the copy of the Coptic translation we have at hand.

The other section probably added after Irenaeus' report is the long revelatory discourse with no interaction between revealer and audience (47,1–53,4). This unit is composed of traditional Sethian material inserted into, and thus interrupting, the dialogue. If Irenaeus had known the document in its present form, he probably would have perceived it as Sethian and classified it accordingly, since he had just dealt with Sethians earlier. Instead, he assigned it to subgroupings that have nothing to do with Sethianism. In terms of sectarian affiliation, the affinity of the Gospel of Judas to Sethianism seems to rest mainly on the surface. In this interpolated section, Jesus discloses the origin of the universe by reporting the sequence of emanations and creations that occurred in the process of establishing the upper and the lower world, but it neither contains the Sophia myth nor the redeemer myth, both absolutely constitutive for Sethianism. The resemblance to other Sethian texts is limited to a mere outline of the main figures, with no interest in their deployment and function, not to speak of any interest in Sethian soteriology (their concepts of salvation) or its baptismal practice. Most of the features are also common in gnostic texts other than Sethian. Even the way Barbelo is mentioned earlier in Judas' confession hardly conforms to Sethian mythology. In Sethianism, Barbelo is the mother in the father-mother-child triad; in Judas' statement, Barbelo is just appended to the word aeon. The name is the only clear Sethian element outside the Sethian section (where Barbelo is not mentioned at all); without it, Judas' declaration would have no Sethian ring to it. Either the name or the entire extension of the confession (see page 159) was probably added when the Sethian unit was inserted sometime after Irenaeus testified to the Gospel of Judas. Still, the familiar Sethian material is so substantially curtailed that it has already lost many of its distinctions from other non-Sethian gnostic texts.

Moreover, the Gospel of Judas, albeit anti-orthodox, is a strong Christian-gnostic text, whereas Sethianism is basically a non-Christian, Jewish-gnostic movement. In general, Sethian writings deal with notorious Old Testament figures by means of reinterpreting their purpose and function in the Hebrew Scriptures, and reassessing their reputation in Judaism; they do not employ New Testament characters. In contrast, *non*-Sethian Christian-gnostic texts favor personages that are marginalized in the orthodox church and give them a different role and meaning. While Sethianism came in contact with Christianity, and its texts were subjected to various degrees of Christianization, the Gospel of Judas apparently went the other way and appropriated Sethian material. Both manners are observed right at the end of the Sethian unit. In a familiar list of archontic angels, the first one is replaced by "Seth," who is then identified with

Christ in a typical way of Christianizing gnostic texts. Yet this is the only Christian feature in the entire cosmological discourse. More importantly, the epithet "Christ" occurs nowhere else in the Gospel of Judas. The fact that it occurs here at all evidences that this entire section was secondarily inserted at a time when it already had been Christianized. Hence, rather than being a document whose Sethian themes are not yet fully developed, the Gospel of Judas in its present form is a late and distant off-shoot of Sethianism.

The Sethian section could have been employed to lend the Gospel of Judas greater authority. In the ongoing quest for accreditation, affiliation with the long-since established and well-attested Sethian system would certainly have strength-ened the claim of the community using the text. The dramatic change in tone of the disciples' vision report—presumably incorporated earlier—suggests that the mutual exclusivity of orthodox and gnostic Christianity must have been fairly well established. Severe disturbances, such as excommunications from Christian communities, may have brought about the adverse attitude toward orthodoxy. Perhaps the polemical but now accredited composition was conducive to the fight against and competition with the orthodox church and could func-tion as a manifesto suitable for usage in the mission field rather than for just devotional purposes within the community.

On the surface, the Gospel of Judas has no interest in redemption and salvation; everyone born mortal is under the control of the erroneous stars and thus destined for eternal doom. Though Jesus reveals knowledge in terms of the origin of the universe and the bliss of the holy generation, everyone here on earth appears to be excluded from that bliss. Yet, the prospect of gnostics is different: They were granted the same knowledge that the supreme God gave to Adam (54,8-12), and the same spirit and soul he gave to the holy generation (53,22-24). Thus, they are exempt from the fateful catastrophe and well equipped to compete in the diverse religious environment of the second century and beyond. By contrast, the apostles and their followers in the orthodox church belong to the doomed generation; they were only given human spirits on loan (53,19-22). Their ignorance is callously exposed in the Gospel of Judas. Even though Jesus told them everything, they still lack the necessary understanding.

Though Judas is portrayed as having an inkling of where Jesus came from, he still remains clueless about everything else. He is just another misguided disciple, hardly known as a gnostic convert. He is undone by his star and will suffer for it. At the end, he will merely have to take his place right above the demonic empire—there is no other way. Rather than Jesus asking him to facilitate the salvation event, he simply has no part in it. Yet, since he was so reviled by orthodox Christianity, the community lying behind the text had granted him a leading role in the dialogue. Instead of adopting the customary portrayal of Judas as traitor, they embrace him in a more sympathetic way. After all, he did not do much harm. His betrayal had no effect on the true Jesus since, by then, his spiritual self, the Christ, was already gone. A proclamation like this is, indeed, good news.

Even though the Gospel of Judas will not turn Christianity on its head or vindicate Judas, it allows us to glance, from a different perspective, at the christological battles that were raging when Christian beliefs were still in flux. Like other ancient books that resurfaced in modern times after having been lost for centuries, the Gospel of Judas facilitates our appreciation of the diverse and intriguing religious environment we call early Christianity.

IRENAEUS OF LYON
AND THE GOSPEL OF JUDAS

Gregor Wurst

CODEX TCHACOS, AN ANCIENT PAPYRUS BOOK FROM EGYPT, ORIGINALLY
contained at least five gnostic treatises, written in the Sahidic
dialect of Coptic, an ancient language of Egypt. First in order
is a badly preserved copy of the Letter of Peter to Philip, a
text already known from the famous discovery at Nag Hammadi, Egypt, in 1945. The second is a much better-preserved
copy of a treatise named "James," which parallels the so-called
First Revelation of James, also found within the Nag Hammadi library. The third is the Gospel of Judas, published here
in a revised English translation. Only parts of the opening
pages survive of the fourth tractate, which has provisionally
been called the Book of Allogenes by the editorial board of
the codex. Finally, there is evidence in a number of additional
fragments not yet reunited with the manuscript that Codex
Tchacos originally contained a Coptic translation of Corpus
Hermeticum XIII. The Coptic language used in the codex is
not the original language of these texts. It is generally assumed
that they were translated from Greek originals, as with all the
Nag Hammadi texts. In the case of the Gospel of Judas, its
name is found in ancient Christian literature, and this essay
investigates a possible link between these ancient references

and the newly discovered text. As a consequence, this link will help us date the Greek original of the Gospel of Judas.

EARLY WITNESSES:
IRENAEUS AND PSEUDO-TERTULLIAN

The existence of a gospel of Judas is first attested by the late second-century bishop Irenaeus of Lyon, who mentions it in his famous treatise *Detection and Overthrow of the False Knowledge,* commonly entitled *Against Heresies.* Although it was originally written in Greek about 180, we possess this treatise only in a fourth-century Latin translation, while fragments of the Greek original survive through citations by later Christian writers addressing the problem of heresy. In appendices to his treatment of the "gnostics" and "other" gnostic believers, called "Ophites" ("Snake People") in later Christian tradition, Irenaeus turns to what he sees to be further subgroupings of these gnostics. He summarizes some of their teachings as follows:

> And others say that Cain was from the superior realm of absolute power, and confess that Esau, Korah, the Sodomites, and all such persons are of the same people as themselves: for this reason they have been hated by their maker, although none of them has suffered harm. For Wisdom [Sophia] snatched up out of them whatever belonged to her. And Judas the betrayer was thoroughly acquainted with these things, they say; and he alone was acquainted with the truth as no others were, and so accomplished the mystery of the betrayal. By him all things, both earthly and heavenly, were thrown into dissolution. And they bring forth a fabricated work to this effect, which they entitle the Gospel of Judas.

According to Irenaeus, this group of gnostics argues for a reevaluation of the Jewish and orthodox Christian ideas of divine salvation. Characters from the Jewish Scriptures such as Esau, Korah, and the Sodomites—regarded by the orthodox tradition as immoral and as rebels against the will of God—are considered here as the servants of the only true God, the "superior absolute power." This power, represented by the gnostic figure of Sophia, is not to be identified with the creator-God of the Judeo-Christian tradition who is called here "their maker."

Even the most malicious figure in the New Testament, Judas Iscariot, the disciple who betrayed Jesus and delivered him to the authorities, is included in this reevaluation. He is regarded by these people as the only disciple—"of all the apostles," according to a Greek citation of this passage by the fifth-century writer Theodoret of Chyrrus—having the knowledge about "these things." Consequently, his deed is presented as a "mystery" leading to the dissolution of all earthly and heavenly things, that is, of all the works of the "maker" or ruler of this world.

From the beginning of the third century on, this group of gnostics was called "Cainites" ("followers of Cain") by Christian writers such as Clement of Alexandria. But most of these later Christian writers are simply dependent on Irenaeus' account. Only the third-century anonymous Latin treatise *Against All Heresies*, falsely ascribed to the early Christian writer Tertullian, and the account of the fourth-century Greek heresiologist (heresy hunter) Epiphanius of Salamis offer supplemental and more detailed information about the alternate view of Judas' act of betrayal within this circle—presumably going back to a lost heresiological treatise of Hippolytus of Rome. In chapter 2 of his treatise, Pseudo-Tertullian characterizes the teachings of the Cainites:

> Moreover, there has broken out another heresy, which is called
> that of the Cainites. And the reason is, that they magnify Cain

as if he had been conceived of some potent virtue which oper-
ated in him; for Abel had been procreated after being conceived of
an inferior virtue, and accordingly had been found inferior. They
who assert this likewise defend the traitor Judas, telling us that he
is admirable and great, because of the advantages he is vaunted to
have conferred on humanity; for some of them think that thanksgiving is to be rendered to Judas on this account: Judas, they say,
observing that Christ wished to subvert the truth, betrayed him,
in order that there might be no possibility of truth's being sub-
verted. And others thus dispute against them, and say: Because
the powers of this world were unwilling that Christ should suffer,
lest through his death salvation should be prepared for mankind,
he, consulting for the salvation of humanity, betrayed Christ, in
order that there might be no possibility at all of the salvation being
impeded, which was being impeded through the virtues which
were opposing Christ's passion; and thus, through the passion of
Christ, there might be no possibility of the salvation of humanity
being retarded.

According to this text, the Cainites held two interpretations of the act of Judas. On the one hand, they are said to
hold the opinion that Jesus was prevented from "subverting
the truth" by the betrayal, a view that remains very obscure for
us and may be regarded as a typical distortion of an orthodox
Christian writer who regarded this portrayal of Judas' deed as
blasphemous. According to the other interpretation, Christ
has been delivered to his death in order to enable salvation
for humanity, which the "powers of this world"—that is, the
inferior forces of the demiurge—were willing to impede. This
statement is similar to what Irenaeus says about the "mystery
of the betrayal" leading to the dissolution of the works of the
inferior powers.

It is important to note, however, that Pseudo-Tertullian does not mention the Gospel of Judas at all. His discussion is limited to what he believes to be the teachings of the Cainites. So that poses the question of whether we should regard the Gospel of Judas, mentioned by Irenaeus, as a Cainite work containing this kind of reevaluation of salvation, or not. If so, the identification of Irenaeus' Gospel of Judas with the text within Codex Tchacos will be difficult, because in the newly discovered text there is no mention of Cain or the other anti-heroes from the Jewish Scriptures mentioned by Irenaeus. As a result, we would have to assume the existence of more than one Gospel of Judas circulating within gnostic communities in antiquity.

HISTORICAL CONTENT OF IRENAEUS' ACCOUNT

Careful analysis of the account of Irenaeus shows that he does not count the Gospel of Judas among the writings originating among these "other" gnostics. He certainly knew of writings composed within that circle, as he states in the next sentence following the above citation: "I have also made a collection of their writings." But regarding the Gospel of Judas he states only that these people "bring forth" or "adduce" a "fabricated work" of that title in support of their view. This assertion implies merely that his opponents referred to a Gospel of Judas to uphold their view of the betrayer as someone endowed with special knowledge and destined to play an important role within their view of divine salvation; it does not necessarily imply that the gospel contained their entire view of salvation.

If this is correct, it is very uncertain that Irenaeus really knew the text of the gospel his opponents are alluding to. On the contrary, unlike the Cainite writings Irenaeus personally collected, he seemed to know the Gospel of Judas only from hearsay. For that reason we cannot be sure in exactly what part of their teachings quoted the Gospel of Judas for support, with the exception of what they called the "mystery of the betrayal."

What can be deduced from the account of Irenaeus with certainty is that the Cainites read a Gospel of Judas and that they referred to it to support their understanding of the act of the betrayal as a mystery. This implies that Judas was portrayed in that gospel as the disciple of Jesus "acquainted with the truth as no others were" and that the act of the betrayal must have been interpreted, in terms of a gnostic view of history of salvation, as part of the "dissolution of all earthly and heavenly things."

COMPARISON OF THE COPTIC GOSPEL OF JUDAS WITH IRENAEUS' ACCOUNT

These two thoughts run throughout the new Coptic Gospel of Judas. From the beginning, Judas Iscariot is portrayed as a disciple having a special knowledge about Jesus' true identity. He appears for the first time on page 35, where he is presented as the only disciple who is able to allow his inner, spiritual personality to come to expression before Jesus. In the same scene, Judas confesses to knowing who Jesus really is and where he comes from: "You have come from the immortal aeon of Barbelo," he says. "And I am not worthy to utter the name of the one who has sent you." And because Jesus knows that Judas is also reflecting upon "the rest (of the things) that are exalted," he exhorts him to part from the disciples and regards him as the only one to be introduced into the "mysteries of the kingdom" (Gospel of Judas 35, 45). So it is to Judas alone whom Jesus will later disclose the knowledge of the "great and boundless aeon, whose extent no generation of angels could (?) see, [in] which is the great invisible Spirit, which no eye of an [angel] has ever seen, no thought of the heart has ever comprehended, and it was never called by any name" (47). What follows is the narration of the entire cosmological myth, ending with the creation of humanity by inferior gods (52-53).

All of this is in perfect accordance with the assertion of Irenaeus that the Judas of his Gospel of Judas is really "acquainted with the truth" as no other disciple of Jesus is. In fact, our new Coptic text presents him as the one to whom "everything has been told" (57). At the end, Judas *is* the perfect gnostic to whom the mysteries of cosmogony have been taught.

With regard to the place of Judas and his betrayal in the history of salvation, our new Coptic text is unfortunately not as clear. This is mainly due to extensive damage on the upper parts of the last pages. On pages 55-57 we can decipher some kind of prophecy from the mouth of Jesus about Judas' act, but several of the most important statements are broken away. The text reads:

> But you will exceed all of them. For you will sacrifice the man who bears me. Already your horn has been raised, and your wrath has been kindled, and your star has passed by, and your heart has [become strong]. Truly [I say to you] your last [. . . , . . .] become [—*about two and a half lines missing*—grie]ving [—*about two lines missing*—] the ru[ler], since he will be destroyed. [And] then will the image of the great generation of Adam be exalted, for prior to heaven, earth, and the angels, that generation, which is from the aeons, exists. Look, you have been told everything. (56-57)

This is clearly prophetic language. Jesus teaches Judas that he will have to play his part in the history of salvation, as he did earlier in the text when he announced that Judas would be replaced be someone else and would be cursed by the other disciples (36, 46). Judas' task is to sacrifice the body of Jesus. Why he has to do this is not preserved, but we may guess that by this sacrifice the inner spirit of Jesus will be liberated. But this cannot be the whole story, because after a gap of about four and a half lines, the text states that "the ruler . . . will be destroyed" and that the "image of the great generation of Adam" will be exalted. On page 55 Jesus had already stated that it is the "stars," which are wandering about with their "five combatants," that "will be destroyed along with their creatures." So not only this world ("their creatures") will be destroyed, but also the powers that guide this world (the "ruler" along with the "stars" and the "combatants"). At the end, the "great generation of Adam," that is, the generation before Seth, will be saved. All this is also included in the word of Jesus that Judas has "been told everything."

It is important to notice that our newly discovered text mentions the destruction of heavenly (the "archon," the "stars," and the "combatants") and earthly realities ("their creatures") in the context of the act of the betrayal of Judas. Even if substantial parts of the text of our new gospel are lost in this passage, we can find here a close parallel to the statement of Irenaeus that by the act of Judas "all things, both earthly and heavenly, were thrown into dissolution."

Given the fact that the Gospel of Judas that Irenaeus is discussing is certainly not a work written within the group of Irenaeus' opponents, given furthermore that he does not seem to have personal knowledge of it, but is only reporting what he knows from hearsay, a link between the new

Coptic text from Codex Tchacos with the Gospel of Judas known from Irenaeus' account seems to be justified. We have seen that in the Coptic text Judas is presented as the only disciple of Jesus endowed with knowledge, and we also find in the text points that can be paralleled with Irenaeus' statement that "all things, both earthly and heavenly, were thrown into dissolution." On this basis, and because we have no evidence to suppose that more than one Gospel of Judas circulated in antiquity, we can be confident in saying that the Gospel of Judas mentioned by Irenaeus is an earlier version of the newly discovered Coptic Gospel of Judas. Consequently, we can assign a date prior to which the gospel had already been written in its original Greek: The Gospel of Judas had been written before 180, when Irenaeus noted that some of his opponents had mentioned it in support of their teachings.

The next question is *how long* before this date the Gospel of Judas was composed. This is very difficult to say, because we neither know its author nor have any detailed historical information about the Christian sect in which it originated. But one fact that can be stated with certainty is that the Gospel of Judas refers to the book of Acts from the New Testament. On page 36, Jesus says to Judas: "For someone else will replace you, in order that the twelve [disciples] may again come to completion with their God"—a clear allusion to the selection of Matthias to replace Judas in the circle of the twelve disciples (Acts 1:15-26). Since the book of Acts is generally dated about 90-100 by scholars of the New Testament, the Gospel of Judas must be placed in the second century. As a consequence, we cannot find here any more accurate historical information about Judas Iscariot than we find in the canonical gospels.

DATE OF CODEX TCHACOS

Since we do not have the original Greek text of the Gospel of Judas, we have to try to determine the date of the copy of its Coptic translation contained in Codex Tchacos. Since the codex was not found by archaeologists during a scientific excavation—in which case its date could be determined with a high degree of certainty—we can only apply the traditional method of comparing its design and the form of writing with other datable papyrus codices, such as those preserved within the Nag Hammadi library. This indicates a date in the first half of the fourth century CE, but dating manuscripts by this method is a delicate task and the degree of uncertainty remains high. A carbon-14 analysis executed by A. J. Timothy Jull from the University of Arizona dated the codex to around the last quarter of the third century (give or take a few decades). This dating may be confirmed by the investigation of the papyrus scraps (called cartonnage) used in the binding, or spine, of the codex, since such scraps—for example, tax receipts or other legal documents—normally are dated. But these papyrus scraps still have to be restored.

CONCLUSION

If this identification of the Gospel of Judas found in Codex Tchacos with the gospel Irenaeus mentioned is convincing, it will be an important step in the study of ancient gnosticism. Most of the Coptic texts from the Nag Hammadi library are extremely difficult to date. Even in the case of the Secret Book of John, a text attested in different versions in four Coptic manuscripts and by a comment of Irenaeus, ranking the priority of this or that version is far from being settled. But if the Gospel of Judas published here is the one in Irenaeus, we would have for the first time the chance to trace back the history of Sethian gnosticism to before the time of Irenaeus.

In the case of this gospel, we have no reason to assume a complex history of editing, because it does not show the marks of subsequent reworking. This is not to say that textual alterations were not made while it was written. But there is no sign that extra parts, such as the revelation of the cosmology (Gospel of Judas 47-53), were written in as later additions. This kind of literary criticism would obviously destroy the original text.

If this text is identified as a Coptic translation of the Greek original mentioned by Irenaeus, the important result of such an identification is that this version of Sethian cosmology also predates 180. So, this new text may possibly supply proven historical evidence that Sethian gnosticism is a movement prior to Irenaeus. This would be a significant gain in our knowledge of early Christianity.

NOTES

THE ALTERNATIVE VISION OF THE GOSPEL OF JUDAS

PAGE 80 . . . *Judas made it all possible* . . . For a radically different interpretation of the Gospel of Judas, in which Judas is indeed the arch-fiend of the text rather than the one who both knows Jesus and attains ultimate salvation, see the discussion of April D. DeConick, *The Thirteenth Apostle: What the Gospel of Judas Really Says* (New York: Continuum, 2007). DeConick's view has been effectively refuted, in my judgment, by Marvin Meyer in his article "The Thirteenth Daimon: Judas and Sophia in the Gospel of Judas," found on Meyer's Web site: *http://www.chapman.edu/meyer*. See also the essay by Meyer, pages 125-154 in the present volume. For a fuller exposition of the views that I lay out here, see Bart D. Ehrman, *The Lost Gospel of Judas Iscariot: A New Look at Betrayer and Betrayed* (New York: Oxford University Press, 2006).

PAGE 87 . . . *the secret knowledge that Jesus is about to reveal* . . . When Jesus informs Judas that "you will not ascend on high to the holy [generation]" (46-47) I take it to mean that he will not ascend while he is still in his mortal flesh, since later in the text Judas *does* have a vision in which he enters into the luminous cloud (57).

PAGE 92 . . . *"but you find him among them [as a child]"* . . . The phrase "as a child" is left untranslated in the English translation of the new critical edition and in the present volume; the Coptic word is unknown, but may be related either to the word "child" or, less likely, "an apparition." In either case this appears to be an indication of what I am here calling a "docetic" Christology, because Christ is said to have assumed some appearance other than his own.

PAGE 98 *... the many people you lead astray ...* This passage is the key text for the provocative interpretation of the Gospel of Judas by Elaine Pagels and Karen L. King, *Reading Judas: The Gospel of Judas and the Shaping of Christianity* (New York: Viking, 2007).

JUDAS AND THE GNOSTIC CONNECTION

PAGE 125 *... Irenaeus of Lyon ...* On the heresiologists and the Gospel of Judas, see the essay by Gregor Wurst. Here and below, the references are to Irenaeus, *Against Heresies* 1.31.1. For a translation of Irenaeus and other heresiological texts against the so-called gnostics, see Werner Foerster, ed., *Gnosis: A Selection of Gnostic Texts,* (Oxford, U.K.: Clarendon Press, 1972, 1974), 1:34-120; and Bentley Layton, *The Gnostic Scriptures: A New Translation with Annotations and Introductions* (Garden City, NY: Doubleday, 1987), 159-214.

PAGE 125 *... "knowers" or "people of knowledge" ...* On the use of the word *gnostic* and related terms, and the nature of gnostic thought, see Bentley Layton, *Gnostic Scriptures* (New York: Doubleday, 1995); Bentley Layton, "Prolegomena to the Study of Ancient Gnosticism," in L. Michael White and O. Larry Yarbrough, eds., *The Social World of the First Christians: Essays in Honor of Wayne A. Meeks* (Minneapolis: Fortress, 1995), 334-50; Antti Marjanen, ed., *Was There a Gnostic Religion?* Publications of the Finnish Exegetical Society 87 (Helsinki: Finnish Exegetical Society; Göttingen: Vandenhoeck & Ruprecht, 2005); Marvin Meyer, *The Gnostic Discoveries,* 38-43; Marvin Meyer, *The Gnostic Gospels of Jesus: The Definitive Collection of Mystical Gospels and Secret Books about Jesus of Nazareth* (San Francisco: HarperSanFrancisco, 2005), x-xiii; Marvin Meyer, "Gnosticism, Gnostics, and the Gnostic Bible," in Willis Barnstone and Marvin Meyer, eds., *The Gnostic Bible* (Boston: Shambhala, 2003), 1-19; Birger A. Pearson, *Gnosticism and Christianity in Roman and Coptic Egypt,* Studies in Antiquity and Christianity (New York: Clark International, 2004), 201-23; and Kurt Rudolph, *Gnosis: The Nature and History of Gnosticism,* English translation, edited by Robert McLachlan Wilson (San Francisco: HarperSanFrancisco, 1987).

PAGE 125 . . . *covering many different types of beliefs* . . . See Karen L. King, *What Is Gnosticism?* (Cambridge, MA: Belknap Press/Harvard University Press, 2003) and Michael A. Williams, *Rethinking "Gnosticism": An Argument for Dismantling a Dubious Category* (Princeton, NJ: Princeton University Press, 1996).

PAGE 126 . . . *groups that are related to Sethian gnostics* . . . See Hans-Martin Schenke, "The Phenomenon and Significance of Sethian Gnosticism," in Bentley Layton, ed., *The Rediscovery of Gnosticism: Proceedings of the International Conference on Gnosticism at Yale, New Haven, Connecticut, March 28-31, 1978*, Studies in the History of Religions (Supplements to *Numen*) 41 (Leiden: E. J. Brill, 1980-1981), 2:588-616; Hans-Martin Schenke, "Das sethianische System nach Nag-Hammadi-Handschriften," in Peter Nagel, ed., *Studia Coptica* (Berlin: Akademie Verlag, 1974), 165-72; John D. Turner, "Sethian Gnosticism: A Literary History," in Charles W. Hedrick and Robert Hodgson Jr., eds., *Nag Hammadi, Gnosticism, and Early Christianity* (Peabody, MA: Hendrickson, 1986), 55-86; John D. Turner, *Sethian Gnosticism and the Platonic Tradition*, Bibliothèque copte de Nag Hammadi, Section "Études" 6 (Sainte Foy, Québec: Presses de l'Université Laval; Louvain, Belgium: Peeters, 2001); and Michael A. Williams, "Sethianism," in Antti Marjanen and Petri Luomanen, eds., *A Companion to Second-Century "Heretics,"* Supplements to *Vigiliae Christianae* 76 (Leiden: E. J. Brill, 2005), 32-63.

PAGE 126 . . . *Nag Hammadi texts* . . . On the Nag Hammadi library, see Jean-Pierre Mahé and Paul-Hubert Poirier, eds., *Écrits gnostiques*, Bibliothèque de la Pléiade (Paris: Gallimard, 2007); Marvin Meyer, *The Gnostic Discoveries: The Impact of the Nag Hammadi Library* (San Francisco: HarperSanFrancisco, 2005); Marvin Meyer, ed., *The Nag Hammadi Scriptures: The International Edition* (New York: HarperOne, 2007); James M. Robinson, ed., *The Nag Hammadi Library in English*, 3rd ed. (San Francisco: HarperSanFrancisco, 1988); and Hans-Martin Schenke, Hans-Gebhard Bethge, and Ursula Ulrike Kaiser, eds., *Nag Hammadi Deutsch*, 2 vols., Die Griechischen Christlichen Schriftsteller der ersten Jahrhunderte, Neue Folge 8, 12 (Berlin: Walter de Gruyter, 2001, 2003).

PAGE 126 . . . *The central confession of Judas Iscariot* . . . It is Peter who offers a confession of who Jesus is in the New Testament synoptic gospels;

see Matthew 16:13-20, Mark 8:27-30, and Luke 9:18-21. When Jesus asks his disciples who people say he is, Matthew has the disciples answer that some say Elijah and others Jeremiah or another prophet, and Peter says, "You are the Christ, the son of the living God"; Mark has Peter saying, "You are the Christ," and Luke has "God's Christ." See also the profession of the disciples in Gospel of Judas 34. Thomas offers his statement about Jesus in Gospel of Thomas 13:

> Jesus said to his disciples, "Compare me to something and tell me what I am like." Simon Peter said to him, "You are like a just messenger." Matthew said to him, "You are like a wise philosopher." Thomas said to him, "Teacher, my mouth is utterly unable to say what you are like." Jesus said, "I am not your teacher. Because you have drunk, you have become intoxicated from the bubbling spring that I have tended." And he took him, and withdrew, and spoke three sayings to him. When Thomas came back to his friends, they asked him, "What did Jesus say to you?" Thomas said to them, "If I tell you one of the sayings he spoke to me, you will pick up rocks and stone me, and fire will come from the rocks and consume you."

PAGE 127 . . . ***God as known through the ineffable name*** . . . See W. W. Harvey, ed., *Irenaeus, Libros quinque adversus haereses* (Cambridge, U.K.: Academy, 1857; reprint, Ridgewood, NJ: Gregg, 1965), 221-2.

PAGE 127 . . . ***Many Sethian treatises . . . maker of the phenomenal world*** . . . John D. Turner, *Sethian Gnosticism*, 85. The citation is slightly modified, in consultation with the author.

PAGE 129 . . . ***The One is a sovereign*** . . . The translations of Nag Hammadi texts throughout this essay are my own. See Marvin Meyer, *Gnostic Gospels of Jesus*, and Marvin Meyer, *Nag Hammadi Scriptures*.

PAGE 129 . . . ***and other texts*** . . . Paul writes, in 1 Corinthians 2:9, "But as it is written, 'What no eye has seen and no ear has heard, and what has not arisen in the human heart, what God has prepared for those who love him.'" Gospel of Thomas 17 reads: "Jesus said, 'I shall give you what no eye has seen, what no ear has heard, what no hand has touched, what has not arisen in the human heart.'" The passage from the Prayer of the Apostle Paul is cited in the notes to the translation.

See also Michael E. Stone and John Strugnell, *The Books of Elijah: Parts 1-2*, Society of Biblical Literature Texts and Translations 18, Pseudepigrapha 8 (Missoula, MT: Scholars, 1979).

PAGE 130 ... *The One is* ... *For no one can understand it* ... Allogenes the Stranger includes a passage (Nag Hammadi Codex XI:61-64) that closely parallels this section of the Secret Book of John.

PAGE 131 ... *The Father gazed* ... *who is Barbelo* ... In the shorter version of the Secret Book of John, it is said that Barbelo gazes into the Father, turns to him, and then gives birth to a spark of light (see Berlin Gnostic Codex 8502, 29-30; Nag Hammadi Codex III:9).

PAGE 132 ... *Harmozel, Oroiael, Daveithai, and Eleleth* ... The names and roles of the Four Luminaries are discussed in John D. Turner, *Sethian Gnosticism*.

PAGE 132 ... *passages in the text Eugnostos the Blessed* ... On Eugnostos the Blessed and the Wisdom of Jesus Christ, see Douglas M. Parrott, *Nag Hammadi Codices III,3-4 and V,1 with Papyrus Berolinensis 8502,3 and Oxyrhynchus Papyrus 1081: Eugnostos and the Sophia of Jesus Christ*, Nag Hammadi Studies 27, The Coptic Gnostic Library (Leiden, The Netherlands: E. J. Brill, 1991).

PAGE 134 ... *the God who creates this world* ... On wisdom, including personified Wisdom, in ancient and particularly Sethian thought, see Marvin Meyer, *Gnostic Discoveries*, 57-115.

PAGE 134 ... *Now Sophia* ... *and was misshapen* ... Sophia attempts to imitate the original procreative act of the Father. The account of Sophia giving birth by herself seems to reflect ancient gynecological theories about women's bodies and reproduction. In Greek mythology, the goddess Hera also imitates Zeus and brings forth a child by herself. According to one version of that story, the child is the monster Typhon (*Homeric Hymn to Pythian Apollo* 300-62). According to another, it is the lame deity Hephaistos, whom Hera evicts from Olympus and sends down to the world below (Hesiod, *Theogony* 924-29). In the Secret Book of John, all the evils and misfortunes of this world derive from Sophia's blunder.

PAGE 134 ... *To begin with* ... *deficiency of the aeons* ... Here the Nag Hammadi version of the Letter of Peter to Philip reads as follows:

> To begin with, concerning [the deficiency] of the aeons, this is the deficiency. When the disobedience and foolishness of the Mother

appeared, without the command of the majesty of the Father, she wanted to set up aeons. When she spoke, the arrogant one followed. But when she left behind a portion, the arrogant one grabbed it, and it became a deficiency. This is the deficiency of the aeons. (135)

PAGE 135 . . . *The word deficiency is a key word* . . . The word *šōōt* in the Coptic text of the Gospel of Judas may be translated as either "sacrifice" or "deficiency." This term, understood as "deficiency," and similar words with similar meanings, function as technical terms in Sethian and other texts for the loss of divine light due to the transgression of the Mother.

PAGE 135 . . . *light of the divine within* . . . The Secret Book of John has the following colorful account (quoted here more fully than in the notes to the translation) of how the divine tricks Yaldabaoth, the creator of this world, into blowing divine light and spirit into humanity:

> When the Mother wanted to take back the power she had relinquished to the first ruler, she prayed to the most merciful Mother-Father of All. With a sacred command the Mother-Father sent five luminaries down upon the place of the angels of the first ruler. They advised him so that they might recover the mother's power. They said to Yaldabaoth, "Breathe some of your spirit into the face of Adam, and the body will arise." He breathed his spirit into Adam. The spirit is the power of his mother, but he did not realize this, because he lives in ignorance. The Mother's power went out of Yaldabaoth and into the psychical body that had been made to be like the one who is from the beginning. The body moved, and became powerful. And it was enlightened. At once the rest of the powers became jealous. Although Adam came into being through all of them, and they gave their power to this human, Adam was more intelligent than the creators and the first ruler. When they realized that Adam was enlightened, and could think more clearly than they, and was stripped of evil, they took and threw Adam into the lowest part of the whole material realm. (II:19-20)

PAGE 137 . . . *higher Wisdom is called Sophia or Echamoth* . . . Here the Gospel of Philip reads, "There is Echamoth and there is Echmoth.

Echamoth is simply Wisdom, but Echmoth is the Wisdom of death—
that is, the Wisdom that knows death, that is called little Wisdom."
Elsewhere (see the First Revelation of James, the Book of Baruch, and
the heresiologists), lower Wisdom is named Achamoth, and she may
be considered the daughter of higher Wisdom, Sophia. The names
Echamoth and Achamoth both derive from the Hebrew word for wisdom, Hokhmah; Echmoth means "like death" in Hebrew and Aramaic
('ekh-moth). See Bentley Layton, *Gnostic Scriptures*, 336.

PAGE 137 . . . *"Sophia of matter"* . . . Here the Holy Book of the Great
Invisible Spirit reads, "A cloud [named] Sophia of matter appeared."
This passage is cited more fully in the notes to the translation.

PAGE 137 . . . *are known from other Sethian sources* . . . Other texts, such as
the Secret Book of John, the Nature of the Rulers, and On the Origin
of the World, also refer to the creator of this world as Samael, a name
that means "blind god" in Aramaic.

PAGE 138 . . . *and gives birth to 12 aeons* . . . On Nebro, Hebrew Nimrod, and the Greek Nebrod of the Septuagint, see the notes to the
translation.

PAGE 138 . . . *When his face flashes with fire* . . . On these descriptions, see
the passages cited in the notes to the translation.

PAGE 138 . . . *The fifth is Adonaios* . . . The name Adonaios derives from the
Hebrew *Adonai*, "my Lord," supplied with the Greek masculine ending
-*os*. The figure Adonaios plays a significant role in gnostic literature. See
the Secret Book of John; On the Origin of the World; the Holy Book
of the Great Invisible Spirit; the Second Discourse of Great Seth; and
the Book of Baruch.

PAGE 139 . . . *The presence of "[Se]th* . . . On the names of Seth, Christ, and
Harmathoth here in the Gospel of Judas, see Marvin Meyer, *Judas: The
Definitive Collection of Gospels and Legends about the Infamous Apostle of
Jesus* (San Francisco: HarperOne, 2007), 159-60; and Gesine Schenke
Robinson, "The Relationship of the Gospel of Judas to the New Testa-
ment and to Sethianism, Appended by a New English Translation of
the Gospel of Judas," *Journal of Coptic Studies* 10 (2008): forthcoming.

PAGE 140 . . . *The figure of Seth* . . . On the role of Seth in Sethian and other
texts, see Birger A. Pearson, "The Figure of Seth in Gnostic Literature,"
in Bentley Layton, *Rediscovery of Gnosticism*, 2:471-504; Birger A. Pearson, *Gnosticism and Christianity*, 268-82; Birger A. Pearson, *Gnosticism,*

Judaism, and Egyptian Christianity, Studies in Antiquity and Christianity (Minneapolis: Fortress, 1990), 52-83; Gedaliahu A. G. Stroumsa, *Another Seed: Studies in Gnostic Mythology* (Leiden, The Netherlands: E. J. Brill, 1984); and John D. Turner, *Sethian Gnosticism.*

PAGE 141 ... *According to the Secret Book of John* ... Here the Secret Book of John reads:

> From the Foreknowledge of the perfect Mind, through the expressed will of the invisible Spirit and the will of the Self-Generated, came the perfect human, the first revelation, the truth. The virgin Spirit named the human Pigeradamas, and appointed Pigeradamas to the first eternal realm with the great Self-Generated, the anointed, by the first luminary, Harmozel. Its powers dwell with it. The invisible one gave Pigeradamas an invincible power of mind. Pigeradamas spoke and glorified and praised the invisible Spirit by saying, "Because of you everything has come into being, and to you everything will return. I shall praise and glorify you, the Self-Generated, the eternal realms, the three, Father, Mother, Child, perfect power." Pigeradamas appointed his son Seth to the second eternal realm, before the second luminary, Oroiael. In the third eternal realm were stationed the offspring of Seth, with the third luminary, Daveithai. The souls of the saints were stationed there. In the fourth eternal realm were stationed the souls of those who were ignorant of the Fullness. They did not repent immediately, but held out for a while and repented later. They came to be with the fourth luminary, Eleleth. These are creatures that glorify the invisible Spirit.

PAGE 142 ... *"Adam the stranger," "holy Adam," or "old Adam"* ... On the possible etymologies of Pigeradamas or Geradamas, see Marvin Meyer, *Gnostic Gospels of Jesus*, 312-13.

PAGE 142 ... *This close connection between Adamas* ... Hans-Martin Schenke, *Der Gott "Mensch" in der Gnosis: Eine religionsgeschichtliche Beitrag zur Diskussion über die paulinische Anschauung von der Kirche als Leib Christi* (Göttingen: Vandenhoeck & Ruprecht, 1962).

PAGE 143 ... *"an image instead of an [image]"* ... On the expression "an image instead of an [image]," compare Gospel of Thomas 22:

Jesus said to them, "When you make the two into one, and when you make the inner like the outer and the outer like the inner, and the upper like the lower, and when you make male and female into a single one, so that the male will not be male nor the female be female, when you make eyes in place of an eye, a hand in place of a hand, a foot in place of a foot, an image in place of an image, then you will enter [the kingdom]."

PAGE 144 . . . *Thus the creator spoke . . . blessed and congenial existence* . . . Benjamin Jowett, ed., *Timaeus* (New York: Liberal Arts Press, 1949); also available at Internet Classics Archive, *http://classics.mit.edu/Plato/timaeus.html.*

PAGE 145 . . . *Sethian texts that incorporated these sorts of Platonic themes* . . . On Platonizing Sethian texts, see John D. Turner, *Sethian Gnosticism.*

PAGE 148 . . . *They have surrounded me* . . . The translations from the Pistis Sophia are taken from Carl Schmidt and Violet MacDermot, eds., *Pistis Sophia,* Nag Hammadi Studies 9, The Coptic Gnostic Library (Leiden: E. J. Brill, 1978).

PAGE 149 . . . *Then, again, as to their assertion* . . . The translation from Irenaeus, *Against Heresies,* is taken from Alexander Roberts and James Donaldson, eds., *Ante-Nicene Fathers, Volume 1: The Apostolic Fathers, Justin Martyr, Irenaeus* (Peabody, MA: Hendrickson, 1994).

JUDAS, A HERO OR A VILLAIN?

PAGE 156 . . . *my own translation* . . . The Coptic wording of additional text reconstructions, and explanations for diverging readings, can be found in the *Journal for Coptic Studies* 10 (2008): forthcoming, where my translation of the Gospel of Judas is published.

PAGE 157 . . . *before he suffered* . . . The given verbal expression is usually translated as "before *he celebrated Passover.*" But what reason would there be for Jesus to stop talking three days *before* having the last meal with his disciples? A translation "before *his* passion" does not work either, since it ignores the fact that the Coptic text uses a *verbal* expression.

PAGE 158 . . . *declaration of judgment* . . . In contrast, translating the much-discussed term *apophasis* as "declaration" (instead of "judgment") renders it quite superfluous in the resulting phrase "word of declaration."

PAGE 158 ... *eschatological theme* ... I believe the entire headline to read, "The secret declaration of judgment that Jesus communicated to Judas Iscariot on eight days, (ending) three days before he (allegedly) suffered" (Gospel of Judas 33,1-6).

PAGE 158 ... *he revealed to them* ... Gospel of Judas 33,13-18: "<He> called the twelve disciples and began to speak with them about the mysteries that are *upon* the world, and the things that will happen at the end." Note: The translation "*beyond* the world" goes beyond the scope of the given Coptic preposition and thus presumably beyond the intent of the text. The expression "*upon* the world" has a clear eschatological overtone: What happened to the world at the end is predetermined by how it came into being and what it entails, the mystery to be revealed.

PAGE 158 ... *any real function* ... There is no preparation for any Passover in the last scene; nor is there a "guest room" that would hint at a last meal. The Greek term used just means "dwelling." The translation of *kataluma* as "guest room" in the New Testament (where the guest room as a rented place is distinguished from the house to which it belongs) should not predetermine the meaning here.

PAGE 160 ... *transcendent realm* ... Gospel of Judas 44,8-13: "[Truly,] I say to you, [neither humans], nor angels, [nor] powers will be able to see those [aeons] that [this great] and holy generation [will see]." Note: The restoration "no authorities" is redundant to "powers," and the assumed Coptic word occurs nowhere else in the text. In the Gospel of Judas, humans are certainly part of the doomed cosmic lot belonging to the lower realm.

PAGE 160 ... *he recounts his vision* ... Gospel of Judas 44,24–45,12: "In the vision, I saw the twelve disciples throwing stones at me; they were [vehemently] running [after me]. And I came to the place [to which I followed] you. I saw [a house at this place], but my eyes could not [measure] its size. Venerable people were surrounding it. That house <had a> single room, and in the middle of the house was a [crowd of people who surrounded] you. [Then he beseeched Jesus and said], 'Teacher, take me in together with these people.'"

PAGE 161 ... *replacement for Judas* ... Gospel of Judas 36,1-4: "For someone else will replace you, so that the twelve [stars] shall again be completed through their god." Note: The reconstruction to "twelve [disciples]" is also possible, but the Coptic word for disciples used by the editors occurs nowhere else in the text, and Jesus already said to the twelve disciples that each of them have their own star (see also 42,7-9). These twelve stars are obviously connected to the zodiac signs and thus always have to be complete for the cosmos to function.

PAGE 161 . . . *inhabitants will curse him* . . . There is no mention of the other disciples cursing Judas because they despise him, as the editors allege. Interpreting the Gospel of Judas through the New Testament does not do the text justice, especially since the allusions to the canonical gospels often assume a different meaning.

PAGE 161 . . . *only preside over the archons* . . . Gospel of Judas 46,5-7: "Teacher, could it be that my seed controls (only) the archons?" Note: I do not believe that the meaning of the given Greek verb is "*under* the control of," since Judas just learned that he will rule "over" them; according to gnostic belief, the seed will be gathered in the same dwelling place as their ancestors.

PAGE 161 . . . *to comfort him again* . . . Gospel of Judas 46,8-14: "Come, and I [shall speak (again) with you about the mysteries of the kingdom. It is possible that you may go there], but you may be greatly groaning when you see the kingdom together with its entire generation."

PAGE 161 . . . *erroneous stars that control* . . . Gospel of Judas 45,24–46,4: "Behold, I have told you the mysteries of the kingdom, and I have taught you [about] the error of the stars and [the] twelve [archons who rule] over the twelve aeons."

PAGE 161 . . . *the other disciples* . . . Hence, there is no need to assume a scribal error and amend the text to "<They> departed"; it is Jesus who departs repeatedly even without clear chronological indications.

PAGE 162 . . . *cosmic destruction* . . . Gospel of Judas 44,2-7: "[This] is the way they [will perish] together with the [aeon] of the [defiled] race and the perishable Sophia, [and] the hand that created mortal people—their souls will <not> go up to the aeons on high." Note: The emendation to <not> is indispensable since the immediate context clearly suggests a negative outcome; nobody would expect the demiurge ("the hand that has created mortal people") to ascend to the highest realm.

PAGE 162 . . . *link between the two figures* . . . To repeatedly refer to Sophia in the Pistis Sophia as the "Wisdom of God" in order to elevate Judas'

192 THE GOSPEL OF JUDAS

image is misleading at best. Marvin Meyer's comparison in this book appears to be an attempt to rescue Judas' initial portrayal. Yet, apart from the fact that the Pistis Sophia is a Valentinian text (whereas the claim for the Gospel of Judas is Sethian), the role of the fallen Sophia there is very different from the way she is, however briefly, depicted in the Gospel of Judas.

PAGE 163 ... *Jesus who enters it*... In order to strengthen the argument for Judas ascending into the cloud, this scene may be compared to a similar scene in the Book of Allogenes 60-61 immediately following the Gospel of Judas in the Codex Tchacos. Yet there Allogenes decidedly does not enter the cloud; he can barely look at it, but only hears the voice above him: "And I heard a word from the cloud and the light, and it shone upon me" (Book of Allogenes 62,15-18).

PAGE 163 ... *an approving crowd*... Gospel of Judas 38,6-13: "A crowd was waiting at that altar, [until] the priests [came out, bringing cattle as] offerings. . . . [Jesus said], 'What kind of [crowd]?'" Note: The text reconstruction to "the priests [finished presenting] the offerings" leaves the remark "the cattle brought in for sacrifice you have seen" in the passage 39,18-40,1, where Jesus repeats what the disciples saw, without a precursor to refer back to.

PAGE 163 ... *sacrificing and unmistakably commands* ... Gospel of Judas 41,1-6: "Stop [sacrificing cattle] that you have [brought] up on the altar, since they are for your stars and their angels, having already died there."

PAGE 164 ... *topic is resumed*... Gospel of Judas 54,24–55,3: "Then they will fornicate in my name, and slay their children, and [lie with men, and commit (other) sins and lawless deeds in my name]."

PAGE 164 ... *who offer sacrifices*... Gospel of Judas 56,11-21: "Truly, [I] say to you, Judas, those [who] offer sacrifices to Saklas [who is called . . . (they do)] everything wicked. Yet you will do more than all of them. For the man who carries me, you will sacrifice."

PAGE 165 ... *assigned it to subgroupings* ... Besides, we do not have to insist on the document at hand being identical with the version mentioned by Irenaeus simply for tracing back the history of Sethian gnosticism to the time of Irenaeus; in the so-called Berlin Coptic Book of the early second century, one fragment quotes parts of a Sethian text and mentions, after the citation, that "this [is the doctrine] of the

Sethians." Hence, the existence of Sethianism is witnessed even before Irenaeus. See Gesine Schenke Robinson, *Das Berliner "Koptische Buch" (P 20915),* CSCO 610 and 611 (2004), esp. 256-257 in vol. 610 as well as XII-XV and 130 in vol. 611.

PAGE 166 . . . *do not employ* . . . The Secret Book of John seems to contradict this assertion, but John occurs only in the framework that secondarily Christianizes the document.

IRENAEUS OF LYON AND THE GOSPEL OF JUDAS

PAGE 169 . . . *written in the Sahidic dialect of Coptic* . . . Coptic is the language of Egyptian Christianity and the last phase of the Egyptian language—that is, the language of the pharaohs—written with the letters of the Greek alphabet plus some additional letters derived from Demotic, a cursive form of writing the hieroglyphic script. Sahidic is one of the two main dialects of the Coptic language.

PAGE 169 . . . *the Book of Allogenes* . . . Photographs of the main parts of the first four pages of this text, together with photographs of the last two pages of the Gospel of Judas, have circulated during recent years among scholars. This led to the impression that the four pages also form part of the gospel. However, the codicological analysis of the manuscript has proven that these pages are the opening part of a fourth tractate whose badly preserved title may be restored as "The B[ook of Allogenes]."

PAGE 170 . . . *treatment of the "gnostics"* . . . On the significance of the terms gnosis and gnostics, see the essay by Marvin Meyer on pages 125-154.

PAGE 170 . . . *And others say that Cain . . . which they entitle the Gospel of Judas* . . . English translation by Bentley Layton, *The Gnostic Scriptures: A New Translation with Annotations and Introductions* (Garden City, NY: Doubleday, 1987), 181 (slightly adapted).

PAGE 170 . . . *Esau, Korah, and the Sodomites* . . . For Esau, see Genesis 25:19-34, 27:32-33; for Korah, Genesis 36:5 and Numbers 16-17; and for the Sodomites, Genesis 18-19.

PAGE 171 . . . *this group of gnostics was called "Cainites"* . . . See Birger A. Pearson, *Gnosticism, Judaism, and Egyptian Christianity, Studies in*

Antiquity and Christianity (Minneapolis: Fortress, 1990), 95-107. Pearson argues that a particular Cainite sect of gnostics never existed in antiquity. According to him, "The Cainite system of gnosis, delineated as such by the heresiologists, is nothing but a figment of their imagination, an artificial construct."

PAGE 171 . . . ***dependent on Irenaeus' account*** . . . For the most complete survey of ancient Christian sources relating to the Cainites and to the Gospel of Judas, see the article by Clemens Scholten, "Kainiten," in *Reallexikon für Antike und Christentum* (Stuttgart: Anton Hiersemann, 2001), 19:972-73; see also Wilhelm Schneemelcher, ed., *New Testament Apocrypha* (English translation edited by Robert McLachlan Wilson; rev. ed.; Cambridge, England: James Clarke; Louisville, KY: Westminster/John Knox, 1991-92), 1:386-7.

PAGE 171-172 . . . ***Moreover, there has broken*** . . . Translation from Alexander Roberts and James Donaldson, eds., *Ante-Nicene Fathers: Translations of the Writings of the Fathers down to A.D. 325* (Buffalo, NY: Christian Literature Publishing Company, 1885-96; reprint, Peabody, MA: Hendrickson, 1994), 3:651 (slightly adapted).

PAGE 173 . . . ***more than one Gospel of Judas*** . . . As it is the case with the famous Gospel of Thomas, also known mainly through a Coptic translation in Nag Hammadi Codex II, 2. In addition to that, another Gospel of Thomas is extant, which belongs to the so-called infancy gospels and whose content is completely different from the Nag Hammadi text.

PAGE 173 . . . ***among these "other" gnostics*** . . . As rightly pointed out by Clemens Scholten ("Kainiten," 975). Scholten even asked whether the last sentence of Irenaeus' account presupposes the existence of a written Gospel of Judas at all.

PAGE 173 . . . ***"bring forth" or "adduce"*** . . . The Latin word *adferunt*, used by the translator of Irenaeus here, can be translated "they bring forth," "they adduce," or even "they produce," so that interpretation depends heavily on the translation adopted.

PAGE 174 . . . ***all earthly and heavenly things"*** . . . This interpretation is held also by Hans-Josef Klauck; see his "Judas: Ein Jünger des Herrn," *Quaestiones Disputatae* 111 (Freiburg: Herder, 1987), 19-21.

PAGE 178 . . . ***far from being settled*** . . . This situation is owing to the fact that no version of the Secret Book of John transmitted by the different

Coptic witnesses can be identified as the source of Irenaeus in *Against Heresies* 1.29. In fact, the Secret Book of John has undergone substantial editing within its history of transmission, so that every theory identifying this or that textual form as the original depends on substantial literary criticism and thus remains conjectural; see John D. Turner, *Sethian Gnosticism and the Platonic Tradition,* Bibliothèque copte de Nag Hammadi, Section "Études" 6 (Sainte Foy, Québec: Presses de l'Université Laval; Louvain: Peeters, 2001), 136-41.

BIBLIOGRAPHY

Barnstone, Willis, and Marvin Meyer, eds. *The Gnostic Bible*. Boston: Shambhala, 2003.

Bauer, Dieter. "Der 'wahre Jünger Jesu': Zum Evangelium des Judas." *Bibel Heute* 42/165 (2006): 4-5.

Bauer, Walter. *Orthodoxy and Heresy in Earliest Christianity*. Philadelphia: Westminster, 1971.

Bethge, Hans-Gebhard, Stephen Emmel, Karen L. King, and Imke Schletterer, eds. *For the Children, Perfect Instruction: Studies in Honor of Hans-Martin Schenke on the Occasion of the Berliner Arbeitskreis für koptisch-gnostische Schriften's Thirtieth Year*. Nag Hammadi and Manichaean Studies 54. Leiden, The Netherlands: E. J. Brill, 2002.

Borges, Jorge Luis. "Three Versions of Judas." In *Labyrinths: Selected Stories and Other Writings*. New York: New Directions, 1964.

Brankaer, Johanna, and Hans-Gebhard Bethge. *Codex Tchacos: Texte und Analysen*. Texte und Untersuchungen zur Geschichte der altchristlichen Literatur 161. Berlin: Walter de Gruyter, 2007.

Brown, Raymond. *The Death of the Messiah*. 2 vols. New York: Doubleday, 1994.

Brox, Norbert. *Offenbarung, Gnosis und gnostischer Mythos bei Irenäus von Lyon*. Salzburger patristische Studien 1. Salzburg: Pustet, 1966.

Cockburn, Andrew, with photographs by Kenneth Garrett. "The Judas Gospel." NATIONAL GEOGRAPHIC May 2006: 78-95.

Crum, Walter E. *A Coptic Dictionary*. Oxford, U.K.: Clarendon Press, 1939.

Culianu, Ioan. *The Tree of Gnosis: Gnostic Mythology from Early Christianity to Modern Nihilism*. San Francisco: HarperSanFrancisco, 1992.

DeConick, April D. *The Thirteenth Apostle: What the Gospel of Judas Really Says*. New York and London: Continuum, 2007.

Doresse, Jean. *The Secret Books of the Egyptian Gnostics: An Introduction to the Gnostic Coptic Manuscripts Discovered at Chenoboskion*. New York: Viking, 1960; reprint, New York: MJF Books, 1997.

Ehrman, Bart D. *After the New Testament: A Reader in Early Christianity*. New York: Oxford University Press, 1998.

———. *Jesus: Apocalyptic Prophet of the New Millennium*. New York: Oxford University Press, 1999.

———. *Lost Christianities: The Battles for Scripture and the Faiths We Never Knew*. New York: Oxford University Press, 2003.

———. *The Lost Gospel of Judas Iscariot: A New Look at Betrayer and Betrayed*. New York: Oxford University Press, 2006.

———. *Lost Scriptures: Books That Did Not Make It into the New Testament*. New York: Oxford University Press, 2003.

Evans, Craig A. "¿Qué Debemos Pensar del Evangelio de Judas?" *Davar-Logos* 5 (2006): 87-93.

———. *Ancient Texts for New Testament Studies: A Guide to the Background Literature*. Peabody, MA: Hendrickson, 2005.

———. *Fabricating Jesus: How Modern Scholars Distort the Gospels*. Downers Grove, IL: InterVarsity, 2006.

———. *Life of Jesus Research: An Annotated Bibliography*. New Testament Tools and Studies 24. Leiden, The Netherlands: E. J. Brill, 1996.

Evans, Craig A., and Donald A. Hagner, eds. *Anti-Semitism and Early Christianity: Issues of Polemic and Faith*. Minneapolis: Fortress, 1993.

Foerster, Werner, ed. *Gnosis: A Selection of Texts*. 2 vols. Oxford, U.K.: Clarendon Press, 1972, 1974.

Gärtner, Bertil E. *Iscariot*. Translated by Victor I. Gruhn. Philadelphia: Fortress, 1971.

Gagné, André. "A Critical Note on the Meaning of *apophasis* in *Gospel of Judas* 33:1." *Laval théologique et philosophique* 63 (2007): 377-83.

Gathercole, Simon. *The Gospel of Judas: Rewriting Early Christianity*. Oxford, U.K.: Oxford University Press, 2007.

————. "The Gospel of Judas." *Expository Times* 118 (2007): 209-15.

Head, Peter M. "The *Gospel of Judas* and the Qarara Codices: Some Preliminary Observations." *Tyndale Bulletin* 58 (2007): 1-23.

Jonas, Hans. *The Gnostic Religion: The Message of the Alien God and the Beginnings of Christianity*. 2nd ed. Boston: Beacon, 1963.

Kasser, Rodolphe. *Compléments au dictionnaire copte de Crum*. Bibliothèque d'études coptes 7. Cairo: Institut français d'archéologie orientale, 1964.

————. *L'Évangile selon Thomas: Présentation et commentaire théologique*. Neuchâtel, Switzerland: Delachaux & Niestlé, 1961.

————. *Papyrus Bodmer VI: Livre des Proverbes*. Corpus Scriptorum Christianorum Orientalium 194-95, Scriptores Coptici 27-28. Louvain, Belgium: Corpus Scriptorum Christianorum Orientalium, 1960.

Kasser, Rodolphe, in collaboration with Colin Austin. *Papyrus Bodmer XXV-XXVI: Ménandre, La Samienne; Le Bouclier*. Cologny, Switzerland: Bibliotheca Bodmeriana, 1969.

Kasser, Rodolphe, in collaboration with Sébastien Favre, Denis Weidmann, et al. *Kellia: Topographie*. Recherches suisses d'archéologie copte 2. Geneva: Georg, 1972.

Kasser, Rodolphe, and Philippe Luisier. "P. Bodmer XLIII: un feuillet de *Zostrien*." *Le Muséon* 120 (2007): 251-72.

Kasser, Rodolphe, Michel Malinine, Henri-Charles Puech, Gilles Quispel, and Jan Zandee, eds. *Tractatus Tripartitus: Pars I, Pars II, Pars III*. 2 vols. Bern, Switzerland: Francke, 1973, 1975.

Kasser, Rodolphe, in collaboration with Victor Martin. *Papyrus Bodmer XIV-XV: Évangile de Luc, chap. 3-24; Évangile de Jean, chap. 1-15.* Cologny, Switzerland: Bibliotheca Bodmeriana, 1961.

Kasser, Rodolphe, Marvin Meyer, and Gregor Wurst, eds. *The Gospel of Judas.* Washington, D.C.: National Geographic, 2006. (Translated into German, French, Italian, Spanish, Greek, Japanese, etc.)

Kasser, Rodolphe, Marvin Meyer, Gregor Wurst, and François Gaudard, eds. *The Gospel of Judas, Together with the Letter of Peter to Philip, James, and a Book of Allogenes, from Codex Tchacos: Critical Edition.* Washington, D.C.: National Geographic, 2007.

Keerankeri, George. "The Controversy over the Gospel of Judas." *Vidyajyoti Journal of Theological Reflection* 70 (2006): 406-16.

King, Karen L. *The Gospel of Mary of Magdala: Jesus and the First Woman Apostle.* Santa Rosa, CA: Polebridge, 2003.

———. *What Is Gnosticism?* Cambridge, MA: Belknap Press/Harvard University Press, 2003.

Klassen, William. *Judas: Betrayer or Friend of Jesus?* Minneapolis: Fortress, 1996.

Klauck, Hans-Josef. *Judas: Ein Jünger des Herrn.* Quaestiones Disputatae 111. Freiburg, Germany: Herder, 1987.

Klijn, A. F. J. *Seth in Jewish, Christian, and Gnostic Literature.* Leiden, The Netherlands: E. J. Brill, 1977.

Knigge, Heinz-Dieter. "Die Rehabilitierung des Judas. Eine historisch-kritische Beurteilung des 'Judasevangeliums'." *Deutsches Pfarrerblatt* 107 (2007): 665-67.

Krause, Martin, and Pahor Labib, eds. *Die drei Versionen des Apokryphon des Johannes im Koptischen Museum zu Alt-Kairo.* Abhandlungen des Deutschen Archäologischen Instituts Kairo, Koptische Reihe. Wiesbaden, Germany: Harrassowitz, 1962.

———. *Gnostische und hermetische Schriften aus Codex II und VI.* Abhandlungen des Deutschen Archäologischen Instituts Kairo, Koptische Reihe. Glückstadt, Germany: J. J. Augustin, 1971.

Krosney, Herbert. *The Lost Gospel: The Quest for the Gospel of Judas Iscariot.* Washington, D.C.: National Geographic, 2006.

Layton, Bentley. *A Coptic Grammar with Chrestomathy and Glossary: Sahidic Dialect.* Porta Linguarum Orientalium, n.s. 20. Wiesbaden, Germany: Harrassowitz, 2000.

————. *The Gnostic Scriptures: A New Translation with Annotations and Introductions.* Garden City, NY: Doubleday, 1987.

Lüdemann, Gerd. *Das Judas-Evangelium und das Evangelium nach Maria: Zwei gnostische Schriften aus der Frühzeit des Christentums.* Stuttgart, Germany: Radius, 2006.

Maccoby, Hyam. *Judas Iscariot and the Myth of Jewish Evil.* New York: Free Press, 1992.

Mahé, Jean-Pierre, and Paul-Hubert Poirier, eds. *Écrits gnostiques.* Bibliothèque de la Pléiade. Paris: Gallimard, 2007.

Marjanen, Antti, ed. *Was There a Gnostic Religion?* Publications of the Finnish Exegetical Society 87. Helsinki: Finnish Exegetical Society; Göttingen, Germany: Vandenhoeck & Ruprecht, 2005.

Marjanen, Antti, and Petri Luomanen, eds. *A Companion to Second-Century Christian "Heretics."* Supplements to *Vigiliae Christianae* 76. Leiden, The Netherlands: E. J. Brill, 2005.

Markschies, Christoph. *Gnosis: An Introduction.* London, U.K.: T. & T. Clark, 2003.

Meyer, Marvin. *The Gnostic Discoveries: The Impact of the Nag Hammadi Library.* San Francisco: HarperSanFrancisco, 2005.

————. *The Gnostic Gospels of Jesus: The Definitive Collection of Mystical Gospels and Secret Books about Jesus of Nazareth.* San Francisco: HarperSanFrancisco, 2005.

————. *The Gospel of Thomas: The Hidden Sayings of Jesus.* San Francisco: HarperSanFrancisco, 1992.

————. *Judas: The Definitive Collection of Gospels and Legends about the Infamous Apostle of Jesus.* San Francisco: HarperOne, 2007.

————, ed. *The Nag Hammadi Scriptures: The International Edition*. San Francisco: HarperOne, 2007.

Nagel, Peter. "Das Evangelium des Judas." *Zeitschrift für die neutestamentliche Wissenschaft* 98 (2007): 213-76.

Paffenroth, Kim. *Judas: Images of the Lost Disciple*. Louisville, KY: Westminster/John Knox, 2002.

Pagels, Elaine H. *Beyond Belief: The Secret Gospel of Thomas*. New York: Random House, 2003.

————. *The Gnostic Gospels*. New York: Random House, 1979.

Pagels, Elaine H., and Karen L. King. *Reading Judas: The Gospel of Judas and the Shaping of Christianity*. New York: Viking, 2007.

Painchaud, Louis. "À propos de la (re)découverte de l'*Évangile de Judas*." *Laval théologique et philosophique* 62 (2006): 553-68.

Pearson, Birger A. *Ancient Gnosticism: Traditions and Literature*. Minneapolis: Fortress, 2007.

————. "Judas Iscariot and the *Gospel of Judas*." Institute for Antiquity and Christianity Occasional Paper 51. Claremont, CA: Institute for Antiquity and Christianity, 2007.

————. *Gnosticism and Christianity in Roman and Coptic Egypt*. Studies in Antiquity and Christianity. New York: T. & T. Clark International, 2004.

————. *Gnosticism, Judaism, and Egyptian Christianity*. Studies in Antiquity and Christianity. Minneapolis: Fortress, 1990.

Perkins, Pheme. *Gnosticism and the New Testament*. Minneapolis: Fortress, 1993.

Perrin, Nicholas. *The Judas Gospel*. Downers Grove, IL: InterVarsity, 2006.

Piñero, Antonio, and Sofía Torallas Tovar. *El Evangelio de Judas*. Madrid: Vector, 2006.

Plisch, Uwe-Karsten. *Was nicht in der Bibel steht: Apokryphe Schriften des frühen Christentums*. Brennpunkt Bibel 3. Stuttgart, Germany: Deutsche Bibelgesellschaft, 2006.

———. "Das Evangelium des Judas." *Zeitschrift für Antikes Christentum* 10 (2006): 5-14.

Porter, Stanley E., and Gordon L. Heath. *The Lost Gospel of Judas: Separating Fact from Fiction*. Grand Rapids, MI: Eerdmans, 2007.

Pratscher, Wilhelm. "Judas, der wahre Freund Jesu: Das Judasevangelium." *Protokolle zur Bibel* 16 (2007): 119-35.

Puech, Henri-Charles, ed. *Histoire des religions: II, La formation des religions universelles et des religions du salut dans le monde méditerranéen et le Proche-Orient, les religions constituées en Occident et leurs contre-courants*. Encyclopédie de la Pléiade. Paris: Gallimard, 1973.

Robinson, Gesine Schenke. *Das Berliner "Koptische Buch" (P 20915): Eine wiederhergestellte frühchristlich-theologische Abhandlung*. 2 vols. Corpus Scriptorum Christianorum Orientalium 610-11 (Scriptores Coptici 49-50). Louvain, Belgium: Peeters, 2004.

———. *Die dreigestaltige Protennoia herausgegeben, übersetzt und kommentiert*. Texte und Untersuchungen zur Geschichte der altchristlichen Literatur 132. Berlin: Akademie, 1984.

———. "The Relationship of the *Gospel of Judas* to the New Testament and to Sethianism, Appended by a New English Translation of the Gospel of Judas." *Journal of Coptic Studies* 10 (2008): forthcoming.

Robinson, James M. *The Secrets of Judas: The Story of the Misunderstood Disciple and His Lost Gospel*. San Francisco: HarperSanFrancisco, 2006.

———, ed. *The Nag Hammadi Library in English*. 3rd ed. San Francisco: HarperSanFrancisco, 1988.

Rudolph, Kurt. *Gnosis: The Nature and History of Gnosticism*. English translation edited by Robert McLachlan Wilson. San Francisco: HarperSanFrancisco, 1987.

Schenke, Hans-Martin. "Das sethianische System nach Nag-Hammadi-Handschriften." In *Studia Coptica*, edited by Peter Nagel, 165-72. Berlin: Akademie, 1974.

Schenke, Hans-Martin, Hans-Gebhard Bethge, and Ursula Ulrike Kaiser, eds. *Nag Hammadi Deutsch*. 2 vols. Die Griechischen Christlichen

Schriftsteller der ersten Jahrhunderte, Neue Folge 8, 12. Berlin: Walter de Gruyter, 2001, 2003.

Schenke, Hans-Martin, and Rodolphe Kasser, eds. *Papyrus Michigan 3520 und 6868(a): Ecclesiastes, erster Johannesbrief und zweiter Petrusbrief im Fayumischen Dialekt.* Berlin: Walter de Gruyter, 2003.

Schneemelcher, Wilhelm, ed. *New Testament Apocrypha.* 2 vols. English translation edited by Robert McLachlan Wilson. Rev. ed. Cambridge, England: James Clarke; Louisville, KY: Westminster/John Knox, 1991-92.

Scholer, David M. *Nag Hammadi Bibliography, 1948-1969.* Nag Hammadi Studies 1. Leiden, The Netherlands: E. J. Brill, 1971.

———. *Nag Hammadi Bibliography, 1970-1994.* Nag Hammadi Studies 32. Leiden, The Netherlands: E. J. Brill, 1997.

Schwarz, Günter. *Jesus und Judas: Aramaistische Untersuchungen zur Jesus-Judas Überlieferung der Evangelien und der Apostelgeschichte.* Beiträge zur Wissenschaft vom Alten und Neuen Testament 123. Stuttgart, Germany: Kohlhammer, 1988.

Scopello, Madeleine. "Vom Verräter zum wahren Jünger Jesu. Das Evangelium nach Judas." *Welt und Umwelt der Bibel* 45 (2007): 32-35.

Scopello, Madeleine, ed. *L'Évangile de Judas: Le contexte historique et littéraire d'un nouvel apocryphe. Colloque international tenu à Paris, Université de Paris IV-Sorbonne les 27-28 octobre 2006.* Nag Hammadi and Manichaean Studies. Leiden, The Netherlands: E. J. Brill, forthcoming.

Sevrin, Jean-Marie. *Le dossier baptismal séthien: Études sur la sacramentaire gnostique.* Bibliothèque copte de Nag Hammadi, Section "Études" 2. Sainte Foy, Québec: Presses de l'Université Laval, 1986.

Smith, Carl B. *No Longer Jews: The Search for Gnostic Origins.* Peabody, MA: Hendrickson, 2004.

Stroumsa, Gedaliahu A. G. *Another Seed: Studies in Gnostic Mythology.* Leiden, The Netherlands: E. J. Brill, 1984.

Turner, John D. "Sethian Gnosticism: A Literary History." In *Nag Hammadi, Gnosticism, and Early Christianity,* edited by Charles W. Hedrick and Robert Hodgson, Jr. Peabody, MA: Hendrickson, 1986.

————. *Sethian Gnosticism and the Platonic Tradition*. Bibliothèque copte de Nag Hammadi, Section "Études" 6. Sainte Foy, Québec: Presses de l'Université Laval; Louvain, Belgium: Peeters, 2001.

Unger, Dominic J., ed. *St. Irenaeus of Lyons: Against the Heresies, Book 1*. Ancient Christian Writers 55. Westminster, MD: Newman, 1992.

van der Vliet, Jacques. "Judas and the Stars: Philological Notes on the Newly Published Gospel of Judas (*GosJud*, Codex Gnosticus Maghâgha 3)." *The Journal of Juristic Papyrology* 36 (2006): 137-52.

van Oort, Johannes. *Het Evangelie van Judas: Inleiding, Vertaling, Toelichting*. Kampen, The Netherlands: Ten Have, 2006.

van Oort, Johannes, Otto Wermelinger, and Gregor Wurst, eds. *Augustine and Manichaeism in the Latin West: Proceedings of the Fribourg-Utrecht International Symposium of the International Association of Manichaean Studies*. Leiden, The Netherlands: E. J. Brill, 2001.

Vogler, Werner. *Judas Iskarioth: Untersuchungen zur Tradition und Redaktion von Texten des Neuen Testaments und außerkanonischer Schriften*. Theologische Arbeiten 42. 2nd ed. Berlin: Evangelischer Verlag, 1985.

Williams, Michael A. *Rethinking "Gnosticism": An Argument for Dismantling a Dubious Category*. Princeton, NJ: Princeton University Press, 1996.

Wright, N. T. *Judas and the Gospel of Jesus: Have We Missed the Truth About Christianity?* Grand Rapids, MI: Baker, 2006.

Wurst, Gregor. *Das Bemafest der ägyptischen Manichäer*. Arbeiten zum spätantiken und koptischen Ägypten 8. Altenberge, Germany: Oros, 1995.

————. *The Manichaean Coptic Papyri in the Chester Beatty Library: Psalm Book, Part II, Fasc. 1: Die Bema-Psalmen*. Corpus Fontium Manichaeorum, Series Coptica 1, Liber Psalmorum Pars 2, Fasc. 1. Turnhout, Belgium: Brepols, 1996.

————. "War er kein Schurke?" NATIONAL GEOGRAPHIC DEUTSCHLAND May 2006: 81-87.

Yamauchi, Edwin M. *Pre-Christian Gnosticism: A Survey of the Proposed Evidence*. 2nd ed. Grand Rapids: Baker, 1983.

PUBLISHER'S NOTE

WHEN ZURICH ANTIQUITIES DEALER FRIEDA TCHACOS NUSSBERGER
acquired the ancient codex that included the Gospel of Judas
in 2000, it had been for sale for nearly twenty years and carried from Egypt to Europe to the United States. Rodolphe
Kasser, a Swiss expert in such Coptic texts, says he had never
seen one in worse shape: "The manuscript was so brittle
that it would crumble at the slightest touch." Alarmed by
its deterioration, Nussburger turned it over to the Maecenas
Foundation for Ancient Art, to restore and translate the manuscript and, ultimately, to give it to Cairo's Coptic Museum.
The codex project, which combined archaeology, cutting-
edge science, and a subject of cultural interest, was a natural
for National Geographic. The Society enlisted the support
of the Waitt Institute for Historic Discovery, a foundation
created by Gateway founder Ted Waitt to support projects
that improve mankind's knowledge through historical and
scientific exploration. The Society and the Waitt Institute
would work with the Maecenas Foundation to authenticate
the document, continue the restoration process initiated on
the advice of Rodolphe Kasser, and translate the contents of
the codex. But first, conservator Florence Darbre, assisted by

Coptic scholars Kasser and Gregor Wurst, had to resurrect the tattered text.

Someone had rearranged the pages, and the top of the papyrus (with the page numbers) had broken away. A greater challenge: Almost a thousand fragments lay scattered like crumbs. Darbre picked up the fragile pieces with tweezers and laid them between sheets of glass. With the help of a computer, she, Kasser, and Wurst were able to reassemble more than 75 percent of the text in five painstaking years. Kasser, Wurst, Marvin Meyer, and François Gaudard translated the 26-page document, a detailed account of long-hidden gnostic beliefs. Scholars of early Christianity say it is one of the most important recent textual discoveries in gnostic studies. Says Kasser, "This script comes back to light by a miracle."

To be certain of its age and authenticity, the National Geographic Society put the codex through the closest scrutiny possible without doing it harm. This included submitting minute samples of the papyrus to the most rigorous radiocarbon dating process available and consulting with other leading Coptic scholars well versed in the fields of paleography and codicology.

In December 2004, the National Geographic Society hand-delivered the five minuscule samples to the University of Arizona's radiocarbon-dating Accelerated Mass Spectrometry (AMS) lab in Tucson, Arizona.

Four samples were papyrus pieces from the codex, while a fifth was a small section of leather book binding with papyrus attached. No portion of the text was damaged in this process.

In early January 2005, scientists at the AMS lab completed their radiocarbon-dating testing. While individual samples' calibrated ages varied, the mean calendar age for the collection was between CE 220 and 340, with an error margin of plus or minus sixty years.

According to AMS lab director Tim Jull and research scientist Greg Hodgins, "the calibrated ages of the papyrus and leather samples are tightly clustered and place the age of the codex within the Third or Fourth centuries AD."

Since its discovery in the late 1940s, radiocarbon dating has been the gold standard for dating ancient objects and artifacts in fields ranging from archaeology to paleoclimatology. The development of accelerated mass spectrometry technology has enabled researchers to sample many tiny fragments of an artifact, as was done in the case of the codex.

The University of Arizona's AMS Lab is world-renowned for its work—including precision-dating the Dead Sea Scrolls, which enabled scholars to place the scrolls accurately within their correct historical context.

The content and linguistic style of the codex is further evidence of its authenticity, according to leading scholars who have studied it. These experts included Rodolphe Kasser, former professor of the University of Geneva, and a leading translator of the Nag Hammadi library; Marvin Meyer of Chapman University, Orange, California; Stephen Emmel, professor of Coptic studies at the University of Münster, Germany; Gregor Wurst, professor of Ecclesiastical History and Patristics at the University of Augsburg, Germany; and François Gaudard, Egyptologist and research associate at the Oriental Institute of the University of Chicago. Kasser, Meyer, Wurst, and Gaudard were instrumental in the translation of this codex.

According to these scholars, the codex's theological concepts and its linguistic structure are very similar to those found in the Nag Hammadi library, a collection of mostly gnostic texts discovered in Egypt in the 1940s that also date to the early centuries of Christianity.

"This text coheres very well with known ideas of the second century of the Common Era. Even in its fragmentary form it is very interesting—it fits very well into the second century, especially the middle of the century," Meyer said.

Emmel concurs with Meyer's view that the content of the codex reflects a unique gnostic worldview prevalent in the second century. "[To fabricate such a document] you would have to reflect a world that is totally foreign to any world we know today. A world that is fifteen hundred years old. . . . That is very difficult for scholars even who spend their lives studying these things to understand, let alone to create for other people. It would take a real genius to produce an artifact like this and personally I don't think it possible," he said.

"I have no doubt whatsoever that this codex is a genuine artifact of late antique Egypt and that it contains evidence for genuine works of ancient Christian apocryphal literature," Emmel added.

In addition to reflecting a gnostic worldview, the paleographic evidence also supports the codex's authenticity. Emmel—an expert in Coptic paleography (handwriting)—gave this assessment: "It is carefully written by someone who is a professional scribe. The kind of writing reminds me very much of the Nag Hammadi codices. It's not identical script with any of them. But it's a similar type of script."

"The question of whether or not someone in modern times could fake an object like this is for me a non-question—it's out of the question. One would not only have to have genuine material, papyrus, and not simply any papyrus, but ancient papyrus. One would also have to know how to imitate Coptic script from a very early period. The number of specialists in Coptic that know that in the world is very small. You would also have to compose a text in Coptic that is grammatically correct and convincing. The number of people who could do that is even smaller than the number who could read Coptic."

In a further effort to absolutely ensure the codex's authenticity, samples of the ink were sent to McCrone and Associates—a firm well-known for its work in forensic ink analysis. This analysis again confirmed the document's authenticity.

Transmission electron microscopy (TEM) confirmed the presence of carbon black as a major constituent of the ink, and the binding medium is a gum—which is consistent with inks from the third and fourth centuries CE.

Using a method known as Raman spectroscopy, McCrone and Associates was further able to establish that the ink contained a metal-gallic ink component consistent with the iron gall inks used in the third century.

ACKNOWLEDGMENTS

We would like to thank several people who have contributed to the preparation of this new edition of the Gospel of Judas. Our colleagues Simon Gathercole and John Turner reviewed the manuscript of the book prior to publication and offered a series of helpful suggestions. At National Geographic, Garrett Brown served as a very capable editor for this publishing project, and Margo Browning and Tiffin Thompson significantly helped in guiding this book through the stages of production. Over the past couple of years a goodly number of colleagues have provided insights into the translation and interpretation of this challenging text, and we thank them for their input. Many of them are mentioned in the footnotes to the translation. A lively discussion about the Gospel of Judas has emerged, and we look forward to this discussion continuing into the future.

—THE EDITORS

ABOUT THE EDITORS

RODOLPHE KASSER is one of the world's leading Coptologists. He is professor emeritus on the Faculty of Arts at the University of Geneva. Philologist and archaeologist, he published several important Greek and Coptic biblical codices of the Bodmeriana Library (P. Bodmer). He also edited and translated Coptic gnostic texts (Codex Jung) and Coptic Manichaean texts. Since 1965 he has been the head of the archaeological excavations of the Swiss Mission of Coptic Archaeology in the Kellia, an important monastic site in Lower Egypt. Professor Kasser organized the restoration and prepared the *editio princeps* of Codex Tchacos.

MARVIN MEYER, Griset Professor of Bible and Christian Studies at Chapman University, Orange, California, and Director of the Chapman University Albert Schweitzer Institute, is one of the foremost scholars on gnostic literature, the Nag Hammadi library, and texts about Jesus outside the New Testament. Meyer is the author or editor of numerous articles and books, among them *Judas: The Definitive Collection of Gospels and Legends about the Infamous Apostle of Jesus, The Nag Hammadi Scriptures: The International Edition,* and *The Gospel of Thomas: The Hidden Sayings of Jesus.* He is one of the translators of Codex Tchacos.

GREGOR WURST is a professor of ecclesiastical history and patristics at the Faculty of Catholic Theology of the University of Augsburg, Germany. He has published widely on Manichaean texts from Coptic Egypt and from Roman North Africa, where the long debates of St. Augustine with Latin-speaking

Manichaeans of his time originated. Wurst earned his doctorate from the University of Münster, Germany, and a habilitation in theology from the University of Fribourg, Switzerland. He is a member of the editorial board of the Nag Hammadi and Manichaean Studies series for Brill and, collaborating with Rodolphe Kasser, is one of the two editors of the original Coptic transcription of the Gospel of Judas.

FRANÇOIS GAUDARD is an Egyptologist and Research Associate at the Oriental Institute of the University of Chicago, where he specializes in the various phases of the ancient Egyptian language, in particular Coptic and Demotic. He works as a researcher for the Chicago Demotic Dictionary and has been an epigrapher for the Epigraphic Survey, based at Chicago House, Luxor, the field headquarters of the Oriental Institute in Egypt. Gaudard received his M.A. and his Ph.D. in Near Eastern Languages and Civilizations (Egyptology, Coptology) from the University of Chicago. He is currently preparing an edition of an ancient Egyptian drama for publication. Gaudard is one of the translators of Codex Tchacos.

ABOUT THE ESSAY CONTRIBUTORS

BART D. EHRMAN is the James A. Gray Distinguished Professor of Religious Studies at the University of North Carolina at Chapel Hill. He is the author or editor of more than 20 books, including the two-volume *Apostolic Fathers* for the Loeb Classical Library and the *New York Times* bestseller *Misquoting Jesus*.

CRAIG EVANS is the Payzant Distinguished Professor of New Testament at Acadia Divinity College in Nova Scotia, Canada. He is the author of many books, including *Jesus and His Contemporaries, Jesus and the Ossuaries,* and *Fabricating Jesus: How Modern Scholars Distort the Gospels.* Evans has appeared in several television documentaries and regularly speaks on such topics as Jesus, archaeology, and the Dead Sea Scrolls.

GESINE SCHENKE ROBINSON is a founding member of the Berlin team that translated the Nag Hammadi texts, a project director of the Coptic Texts Editing Project at Claremont Graduate University, a professor of New Testament at the Episcopal School of Theology, and an adjunct professor of Claremont School of Theology in Claremont, California. She has published extensively in Coptic Studies and related fields, among others the *editio princeps* of Nag Hammadi Codex XIII,1 and the so-called Berlin Coptic Book.

INDEX

A

Abel 13, 139, 172

Achamoth 187n

Acts (NT book) 7, 84, 177

Acts of John 30n8

Adam: in Genesis 44n106, 133, 140; in gnostic texts 44n106; in Gospel of Judas 44-45, 48, 49, 140, 141, 142; in Secret Book of John 44n106, 49n136, 143, 186n

Adamas (heavenly Adam) 43, 44, 140, 141-142, 188n

Addon 46n118

Adonaios 46n118, 47, 138, 139, 187n

Aeons 45n114, 185n; *see also* Thirteenth aeon

Against All Heresies 171-173

Against Heresies 31n11, 170, 182n, 189n, 195n

Akhmîm fragment 113-115

Akiressina 139

Allogenes (form of Seth) 140, 141, 154; *see also* Book of Allogenes

Allogenes the Stranger (Nag Hammadi Codex): Barbelo in 32n22; ineffability and transcendence of the divine 33n23, 42n92, 130; Secret Book of John parallels 185n; the Self-Generated in 43n97; as Sethian text 140

Andrew: conflicts with Mary Magdalene 117

Angels: in gnostic texts 138-139; in Gospel of Judas 47, 138, 139

Anti-Semitism 15-16

Apocalypses 100

Apocryphon of John 193n

Arai, Sasagu 52n155

Archir-Adonin 139

Athoth 139

Authades 148

Autogenes the Self-Generated: as child of God 43n97, 131, 153; creation role 43n99, 44n105, 128; in Gospel of Judas 43-44, 45, 127, 131, 132; in Secret Book of John 43n99, 131, 188n

B

Bagnall, Roger 66

Barbelo: in Allogenes the Stranger 32n22; in Gospel of Judas 32, 127, 154, 166; in Holy Book of the Great Invisible Spirit 32n22, 45n112; offspring 127, 128, 131, 153, 166; origin of name 32n22, 127; in Secret Book of John 131, 185n; in Sethian cosmology 32n22, 85-86, 91, 126-127, 128, 153, 166; in Three Forms of First Thought 32n22; as virgin 45n112; in Zostrianos 32n22

Barnstone, Willis 183n

Beinecke Library, Yale University 66-67

Belias 139

Berlin Coptic Book 192n

Berlin Gnostic Codex 65, 185n

Bethge, Hans-Gebhard 30n7, 31n14, 182n

Book of Allogenes: comparison to Gospel of Judas 192n; Jesus in 52n156, 141, 154; language of 169; as part of Codex Tchacos 11, 59, 72, 140-141, 169, 193n

Book of Baruch 187n

Books of Jeu 50n146, 147

Brown, Dan 117

Bultmann, Rudolf 109

C

Cain 13, 139, 170, 171-172

Cainites 171-173, 174, 193-194n

Cherix, Pierre 38n62

Christianity: early debates about beliefs 89, 100-101, 167, 179; lost Christianities 120-122; proto-orthodox 98, 99

Clement of Alexandria 118-120, 171

Codex Tchacos: authentication 208-211; condition 2, 22-23, 208; contents 11, 58-59, 65-66, 72, 169; damage 63, 64-65, 66, 67, 70, 72-73; dating 12, 178, 208-209, 210; discovery 10-12, 17, 59-60, 207-208; editions 17, 75; identification of remnants 75-76; language written in 59, 69-70, 169; missing fragments 75; pagination 63, 72-73, 74-75; Paris announcement 75; photographs of 76-77; relationship to Nag Hammadi library 58-59, 209, 210; restoration 68-69, 70-73,

BIBLE INDEX